# We Left
# Jehovah's Witnesses

# WE LEFT
# JEHOVAH'S WITNESSES--

# A Non-Prophet Organization

By
**EDMOND C. GRUSS**

With the testimonies of converted
Jehovah's Witnesses

**Presbyterian and Reformed Publishing Co.**

Religion Analysis Service, Inc.
902 Hennepin Ave.
Minneapolis, Minn.  55403

First printing, June 1974
Second printing, January 1975

Library of Congress Catalogue Card No. 74–78761
*Printed in the United States of America*

# TABLE OF CONTENTS

## ACKNOWLEDGMENTS

I would like to thank all those whose testimonies are recorded in this book for their cooperation and their continuing encouragement. Additional thanks go to William Cetnar and Kenneth Guindon, who supplied many of the photographs, and to Rik, Tom, and Russ, who processed them. My appreciation is also expressed to Prof. John Hotchkiss, who gave many hours of assistance in the editing of the testimonies, to my wife Geraldene, who typed the manuscript, to Clint Crittenden, who designed the cover, and to Ron Vandermey, who proofread the manuscript.

Unless otherwise noted, the Bible quoted in this book is the Authorized (King James) Version. The abbreviation NWT is used for the New World Translation of the Holy Scriptures, published by the Watchtower Bible and Tract Society.

**Edmond Gruss**

Why was this book written? The answer to this question began a number of years ago. I was raised as a Jehovah's Witness for ten years (1940–1950) and was thoroughly convinced of the truth of this system, for I knew nothing else. It was during 1950, just before my graduation from high school, that I was often challenged by some earnest Christian young people and their pastor to accept Christ's free offer of eternal life. At first I steadfastly rejected these invitations, but later, in the privacy of my own room, I responded to Christ and was "born again" (John 3:3, 5, 7; I John 5:1-13). While this decision brought a peace and joy which I never had before, the other teachings that I had accepted as a Jehovah's Witness remained.

Coming free of Watchtower doctrinal error was a gradual process which required several years of earnest prayer and study. During this time I was burdened for other Witnesses.

1

I wanted to tell them of their need of salvation through faith in Jesus Christ and to share with them what I had discovered about the movement which I once believed to be Jehovah God's "prophet"—His visible organization. God gave me a number of opportunities to speak to Jehovah's Witnesses.

The years passed, and after graduation from college and seminary, I desired to write something on the Witnesses. I had long wanted to do this, but to this point nothing of consequence had materialized. In 1958 I determined that it was God's will to go on to further graduate study and to work on the Master of Theology degree, which required the writing of a thesis. My graduate program and a thesis on the Witnesses, were finished in 1961. God blessed the thesis manuscript when several persons who had been studying for years with the Jehovah's Witnesses read it and immediately left the movement. In May, 1970, *Apostles of Denial,* a book based on the thesis, was published. Soon after this, letters from those who had read my book began to come in from all over the world, telling of the book's help and their deliverance. Many were former Jehovah's Witnesses who shared with me their stories of long involvement with the Watchtower organization, their deliverance from it, and their assurance of eternal life through faith in Jesus Christ.

As further contacts were made through *Apostles of Denial,* I thought of the blessing that these testimonies of ex-Jehovah's Witnesses were, and how many people could be helped if they could hear or read them. In late January, 1973, I was contacted by Ken Guindon, who, after sixteen years as a Witness (fourteen years as a full-time worker), was well on his way to deliverance from the cult. Ken and I had several discussions, and after his further prayer and study he decided to leave the movement. Both Ken and his wife Monique were "born again," and they submitted their letter of resignation to their local Kingdom Hall on March 16.

It was at this point that the project of compiling the testimonies of several ex-Witnesses began. I asked Ken to write his testimony and sent out letters requesting some others to do the same. I could have contacted more, but felt God's leading to limit the testimonies to those included here.

I have spoken to or corresponded at length with these writers, and I can say truthfully that what they have written came not from bitterness or hatred, but from concern and love for the Jehovah's Witnesses and those who are in the process of becoming members. Each writer has a heart-felt desire to see others accept the finished salvation in Jesus Christ and to experience the peace, joy, and security He can give—outside the Watchtower Society. To their former brethren and potential Witness converts, each one says with Paul, "Am I therefore become your enemy, because I tell you the truth?" (Gal. 4:16).

## II

## THE JEHOVAH'S WITNESSES: GROWTH AND EXODUS

In the September 1, 1973 issue of the *Los Angeles Herald-Examiner,* UPI Senior Editor Louis Cassals identified the Jehovah's Witnesses as "America's fastest growing religious body. . . ."[1] The movement's growth percentages began to increase after the publication in 1966 of a new date for the completion of 6,000 years of human existence. What was the significance of this Witness calculation?

> . . . Six thousand years from man's creation will end in 1975, and the seventh period of a thousand years of human history will begin in the fall of 1975 C.E. . . . It would not be by mere chance or accident but would be according to the loving purpose of Jehovah God for the reign of Jesus Christ, the "Lord of the sabbath," to run parallel with the seventh millennium of man's existence.[2]

Bill Cetnar, who worked in Witness headquarters for over eight years, observed that Watchtower leadership became uneasy when growth percentages dipped down (3.2% in 1965; 2.4% in 1966, an increase of only 24,407 active members) and that he expected some important announcement would be made in an effort to stop the trend. That important announcement was the 1975 date. The impact of this date became

---

1. P. A-7.
2. *Life Everlasting—in Freedom of the Sons of God* (New York: Watchtower Bible and Tract Society, Inc., 1966), pp. 29, 30.

4

evident in the yearly reports which followed. From a low percentage of 2.4% growth in 1966, percentage increases were: 5.6, 8.7, 10.2, 9.1, and 5.7 for the years 1968–1972. Averages for Witnesses involved in preaching activities went from 1,058,675 in 1966 to 1,656,673 in 1973, for an increase of almost 600,000.[3]

Although the Jehovah's Witnesses have made substantial gains, in 1972 their organization was only third in size among the major cults. The Church of Jesus Christ of Latter-day Saints (Mormons) numbered 3.15 million members, and the Seventh-day Adventists had 2.2 million adherents.[4] When the researcher looks at the expansion of the Witnesses since World War II, the following observation should be kept in mind:

> Thus although the growth of Jehovah's Witnesses *is* impressive considered in isolation, it is more than matched by the expansion of other sects and therefore cannot be used, as the Witnesses use it, as proof that they have the Truth.[5]

What impressed me most in the study of Witness growth statistics was not the rapidity of the group's expansion, but rather the relative gradualness of expansion when viewed in the light of the hundreds of millions of hours spent and the large number of publications distributed in the propagation of this cult's views. For example, during 1972, to bring one

---

3. *Yearbooks*, 1967–1974.
4. *Britannica Book of the Year 1973*, pp. 588, 591. Although the Seventh-day Adventists are used here for numerical comparison together with the Witnesses and Mormons, it is my conviction that many Adventists are truly regenerate people. The Seventh-day Adventist Church is still regarded by many evangelicals as a cult. See Anthony A. Hoekema's *The Four Major Cults* and Norman F. Douty's *Another Look at Seventh-day Adventism*.
5. Alan Rogerson, *Millions Now Living Will Never Die* (London: Constable & Co., Ltd., 1969), p. 76.

5

person to baptism required the efforts of approximately ten *active* Witnesses and almost 1800 hours of service. (These figures are calculated by dividing the number of active Witnesses and hours of service recorded, by the number baptized.) In 1973 the Witnesses had their highest number of baptisms ever, 193,990, yet the average number of active Witnesses increased only a little more than 60,000 over the previous year. This represented a percentage increase for the year of only 3.8 percent.[6]

Over the years, while many were becoming converts to the Watchtower system, hundreds of thousands were also leaving the movement. The departure of individuals or groups has been part of the history of this organization from its beginnings in the 1880's.[7]

In the December 1, 1927, *Watch Tower*, J. F. Rutherford indicated that by that time a majority of the followers of the Society's founder, C. T. Russell, had left the organization.[8] And in 1939 "only a small remnant" of adherents from the Russell years were still in the movement.[9]

Many left the organization during Rutherford's administraion (1917–1942) for a number of reasons. The following two examples serve to illustrate some of these. The accounts are valuable because when Olin Moyle and Harvey Fink left the Society, their reasons were not basically doctrinal, but or-

---

6. *1973 Yearbook*, pp. 30, 31. The average number of publishers in field service during 1972 was 1,596,442, and the number of baptisms was 163,123. There were almost 292 million hours reported. The 1973 figures are found in *The Watchtower*, January 1, 1974, p. 30.

7. I have come across about two dozen Watchtower splinter sects. I am periodically surprised to find some new group or publication which represents a separation from the Watchtower Society. Some of these splinter sects are discussed in my book *Apostles of Denial*, pp. 264-289.

8. Cited in Timothy White, *A People for His Name* (New York: Vantage Press, 1967), p. 251.

9. *The Watchtower*, February 1, 1939, p. 37.

6

ganizational, and from their experiences they seriously questioned the Watchtower Society's claim to being God's "sole collective channel for the flow of Biblical truth to men on earth. . . ."[10]

*Olin Moyle.* Olin Moyle served as legal counsel to the Watchtower Society, without pay, for four years before he resigned. He had been with the movement for more than twenty years when he was "excommunicated" from the Jehovah's Witnesses in March, 1940. After being attacked in the October, 1939, *Watchtower,* Moyle brought suit for libel against Watchtower president Rutherford and the Board of Directors. He won a settlement of $15,000.[11] In the letters which Moyle wrote to President Rutherford and his own Kingdom Hall in Milwaukee, he set forth his position and specified what he found wrong in Rutherford's administration and the organization.

Moyle related to Rutherford why he resigned from his Bethel appointment and specifically mentioned: Rutherford's poor treatment of the Bethel personnel, his excessive anger, his discrimination, the allowance of "vulgar speaking and smut," and the "glorification of alcohol and condemnation of total abstinence. . . ." After Moyle's severance from the Society he again wrote President Rutherford, and he asked him: "Do your commands as president of the Society supersede and set aside the laws of Almighty God?"

In his letter to the Milwaukee congregation dated September 25, 1940, among other things Moyle states:

> The Society's intolerant attitude and practices cannot be reconciled with Christianity. Real Bible study has been gagged and suppressed by the organization. . . . God's

---

10. *The Watchtower,* July 15, 1960, p. 439.
11. David Manwaring, *Render Unto Caesar* (Chicago: The University of Chicago Press, 1962), pp. 222, 306, note 71.

people among Jehovah's witnesses are being ensnared into bondage to a Rutherford Hierarchy which is of the same order and just as intolerant as the Papal machine.[12]

In a trip to Brooklyn, New York, I was able to check the trial transcript folder on the Moyle trial in the Supreme Court Building. The folder contained an interesting dittoed sheet prepared by Olin Moyle, marked "Exhibit D," and titled "God is Not the Author of Confusion." This page presented thirteen obvious contradictions on key doctrines found in Watchtower publications published during the Rutherford era. At the end of these contradictions Moyle asks: "Isn't it blasphemy to attribute this jumble of contradictions to an all wise God? Are not the WATCHTOWER and its followers being blown about with many conflicting winds of doctrine?" To these questions the objective reader must answer in the affirmative.

*Harvey H. Fink.* In a two-page printed document, "An Open Letter to Jehovah's Witnesses," dated September 25, 1940, former zone servant Harvey H. Fink wrote:

> Since 1922 I sincerely believed that only the Watch Tower organization could possibly be pleasing to Almighty God because I, without question, believed the Society's claim that it alone preached the good news of the Kingdom to the people. However, during the past years in my capacity of divisional servant, and later zone servant, I began to notice an unmistakable feeling of unhappy restraint among a goodly number of the friends. Their liberties were being curtailed; they were little by little being denied the privilege of deciding what was truth; they were asked to accept without equivocation what was placed before them.

Fink made a number of other observations drawn from his

---

12. A brief background on the Moyle case and his letters are found in my book, *Apostles of Denial*, pp. 290-299.

intimate experience with the movement, some of which are enumerated here.

1. Similar to the Catholics and like other Bible students before them, the Jehovah's Witnesses were "being molded into just another obedient religious group, without freedom of thought or expression and kept in line through the paralyzing fear that otherwise they will not get through Armageddon."

2. "The Society's regulation of meetings, Scripturally unauthorized, in effect does away with genuine Bible study. What are called studies are mere reading lessons or catechisms."

Fink concluded that

> the Society's attitude is—"prove nothing; hold fast that which the Society publishes and muzzle anyone who dares question or disagree." The reason for gagging these studies is that the Watch Tower will not bear close examination. It distorts Scripture and is full of inconsistencies. To cite all would take a volume.

3. Of Rutherford's writings he stated: "Now one man alone presumptiously concocts what he considers truth and pawns it off as coming direct from the Lord." That Fink's conclusion was correct is easily verified by reading the contradictory statements in the publications of the Rutherford period. Fink also gave some examples.

4. Fink indicated that while he continued to be an active witness of the Kingdom, he did this

> entirely devoid of any coercive 60 hour per month laws set up by presumptious men whose interest in spite of their pretenses to the contrary, is primarily selling books for revenue. . . .

He demonstrated the correctness of his conclusion by pointing out that long after the Society had reversed itself on several key doctrines published in Rutherford's books, "it demanded that these books be sold to the people very definitely, because it wanted to get the revenue out of them in spite of the errors it willingly admitted they contained." This was not the only time when books which contained admitted error were distributed. The Witnesses' *Informant* of April, 1946, under "Literature Presentations," lists most of Rutherford's books as part of a special campaign of literature placement. These books contain many doctrines which the Society had rejected years before. Three examples should make the point: (1) *Life* (1929) considers "the certainty of the promises that Israel shall be returned to Palestine." (2) *The Harp of God* (1921) teaches that "the time of the end" began in 1799 and "the Lord's second presence dates from 1874. . . ." *Vindication*, volume three (1932), and *Preparation* (1933) teach that the "great multitude" was a Spirit-begotten class. Many additional examples could be cited.[13]

William J. Schnell was probably the most well-known defector from the Watchtower Society by reason of his best-selling book, *Thirty Years a Watch Tower Slave* (1956). Among other things, Schnell concluded that the Society employed many of the same methods that it condemned in the Roman Catholic Church and other churches.[14]

One of the most active ex-Witnesses in evangelical circles today is Ted Dencher. Ted left the movement after a ten-year involvement. In his book *Why I Left Jehovah's Witnesses* (1966) he explains how he found salvation in Jesus Christ, he relates his departure from the group, and he exposes its doctrinal errors.[15]

---

13. *Life*, p. 120. *The Harp of God*, pp. 230-237 or 235-241, according to edition. *Vindication*, III, p. 204, *Preparation*, p. 164.
14. (Baker Book House), pp. 179-191.
15. (Christian Literature Crusade). Ted's testimony, "I Left Jehovah's Witnesses!" is on LP record (see the bibliography).

## Where Are the 400,000?

A study of Watchtower publications reveals that during the past twenty-five years over 400,000 persons who were induced to become baptized Jehovah's Witnesses are no longer active in the movement. How can this fact be established?

One of the articles in the March 1, 1967, *Watchtower* asked the question: "Were *You* Once a Kingdom Publisher?" The treatment indicated that after an allowance for deaths in the movement was deducted "it still leaves about 100,000 persons who have ceased to preach in just the past five years."[16] Another article in the September 1, 1969, *Watchtower* queried, "WHERE ARE THE 200,000?" It was estimated that during a twenty-year period (1949 to 1968) there were "nearly 200,-000 who professed to have had enough faith in God that they dedicated their lives to his service, but who somewhere along the line lost their faith and quit preaching."[17]

By following the same method of calculation employed in *The Watchtower* articles above, it can be established that at least 200,000 Witnesses left the movement or were no longer active in it between 1969 and 1973. Adding up the twenty-five year total (1949 through 1973) brings the figure to at least 400,000. The statistics also show that most who left the movement or became inactive did so during the past ten to twelve years.[18]

---

16. P. 150.
17. P. 533.
18. The average number of publishers in the field service during 1969 was 1,256,784 and for 1973 was 1,656,673, which represents an increase of 399,889 for these five years. Baptisms for this same period totalled 792,019, for a difference of 392,130. After deducting a generous 1% each year for deaths in the movement and using the *peak* figure for publishers in 1973 (1,758,429) rather than just the average, it leaves a total of more than 200,000 unaccounted for in these five years.

11

## Where Do They Go?

It is impossible to give accurate figures as to where Witnesses go who leave the movement, but from my experience and that of others who have studied the group, some observations might be made. (1) Many former Witnesses end up as religious skeptics or agnostics. They have the attitude, "If the Witnesses don't have the truth, it cannot be found anywhere." These often reject all religion. (2) Some join other cults, such as the Worldwide Church of God (Herbert W. Armstrong), Adventist splinter groups, and the Mormons. Others have become converts to Judaism. (3) Many leave and become followers of one of the Watchtower splinter groups, such as the Dawn Bible Students, Laymen's Home Missionary Movement, and the Associated Bible Students. Some even start groups of their own. (4) Some go back to their former theologically liberal church affiliations and remain unregenerate. (5) A number find salvation in Christ and are "born again" (John 3:1-17). In many cases being "born again" was their reason for leaving the Witnesses in the first place. These often find their way into evangelical churches. The former Witnesses whose testimonies make up the bulk of this book fall into this category and are typical of the thousands like them who have found "The Truth" in a personal relationship with Jesus Christ. They have found freedom not just from the Witnesses' organization, but true spiritual freedom in God's Son (John 8:32-36).

Guido and Dolly Meneghini

III

**FREE FROM BONDAGE**

by

Dolly Meneghini

I truly thank and praise the Lord for saving me out of the Jehovah's Witnesses. As a child I had practically no religious training, but I was always interested in reading religious literature. I did not know the doctrines of Christianity, but in 1940, about six years after my marriage, my husband and I, and our two-year-old son, began attending the Methodist church in the small town in which we lived. Sometimes my husband did not care to go, so my son and I went alone.

In 1941 a Jehovah's Witness woman came to our house with a phonograph and asked if I would listen a few minutes to a record about the Bible. I cannot now recall what the message was, but I do remember that I didn't understand very much of it. She showed me a book entitled *Children* and told me it was based on the Bible and that I could have it for a

13

small contribution. I bought the book from her, thinking that I was helping some religious organization. After she had gone, I gave the book a cursory examination and set it aside. I didn't think much of it; it was about an engaged couple named Eunice and John who decided to give up getting married because Armageddon was soon to come (see Figures 1 and 2). It didn't make much sense to me, and it wasn't what I had expected from a book supposedly based on the Bible. I put the book away and forgot about it.

Several months later the same woman came back, accompanied by a friend. They asked me what I thought of the book, and I told them what my reaction had been. We engaged in several discussions about religion, world events, church-going, and other topics. I agreed with them on some issues, but disagreed on others. During these discussions we remained friendly with each other. I thought they were very nice people, and they certainly were. As they departed, they presented me with a copy of *The Watchtower* magazine, the first I had ever seen. I read parts of it the next day, but it discussed the Old Testament, and was difficult to understand. After several months, one of the women came back, this time accompanied by her sister. I told them I didn't get anything out of the magazine, but they were very understanding, and our discussions on different issues continued. It was then that I found out that they were against war. So was I! This certainly gave us a great deal in common, or so I foolishly thought. They dropped in from time to time, but not very often, since there was no Kingdom Hall where I lived and the women had to travel from a neighboring town. I told my husband about these discussions and he never seemed to object to the ladies' visits.

After the birth of our daughter in 1943, we moved to another neighborhood, and we didn't see any Jehovah's Witnesses for over six months. By this time we had stopped going to church. When the same two women found us again, they made the suggestion that since I wasn't attending church, it would be good if I would get some Bible knowledge by having a study with them in the book *The Truth Shall Make You Free.* I always felt that my Bible knowledge was shallow, so I consented, thinking how nice they were to take the time to do this. They showed me from the Bible that this was how Christ's disciples had taught the people, and that the Jehovah's Witnesses were the only ones going from door to door with their message. This sounded good to me, and I began to study with them. Again, my husband didn't object. He said that as long as I wouldn't go from door to door it would be all right. When I told the Witnesses this, they said they weren't out to convert people, but just wanted to give them Bible knowledge. I know now that this was a misrepresentation, because their main object is to bring people into their organization.

It took many months to cover the book because there were many weeks when I couldn't have the study, some weeks when they couldn't come, and other times when we were side-tracked by discussions on issues on which we disagreed. They kept inviting me to visit the Kingdom Hall, but I didn't readily agree until a few years later. Most of the people I met there were very nice, and some of them later became some of our closest friends.

In 1946 they suggested I study *Let God Be True*, a book just released that year. I really thought I was learning the doctrines of the Bible. I had a good memory and learned scriptures rapidly—scriptures that were supposed to prove certain doctrines. Little did I know that this is where they (unknowingly) are masters of deception, taking isolated scriptures out of context to support a preconceived theology. Of course, I know now that most of the individuals who come that shall be upon the whole earth during the reign of Christ the King.''

"How true are your words, Eunice. We have walked through these broad fields many times, during our childhood days. But to-day these fields mean much more to us than ever before. They belong to the Lord, and He will beautify them for his children. <u>Armageddon is surely near, and during that time the Lord will clean off the earth everything that offends and is disagreeable</u>. Then, by His grace, we shall begin our life with a greater vision and prolonged joy. Now we see by faith the great THEOCRACY, and we are wholly and unreservedly committed to that righteous government. From now on we shall have our heart devotion fixed on THE THEOCRACY, knowing that soon we shall journey for ever together in the earth. <u>Our hope is that within a few years our marriage may be consummated and, by the Lord's grace, we shall have sweet children that will be an honor to the Lord. We can well defer our marriage until lasting peace comes to the earth</u>. Now we must add nothing to our burdens, but be free and equipped to serve the Lord. When THE THEOCRACY is in full sway it will not be burdensome to have a family. Then we may often walk through these broad fields, amidst the beautiful forests and environments, and will walk with our beloved children by our side and tell them all we have learned from the Lord,

**Figure 1**

Page 366 of J. F. Rutherford's *Children*, published in 1941. At this point in the book twenty-year-old John and eighteen-year-old Eunice agree that "Armageddon is surely near" and they postpone their marriage. Their hope was that "within a few years" (when the Theocracy was in full sway) they could get married. The "few years" have now become thirty-two, and John is fifty-two and Eunice is fifty.

Cartons of *Children* that had been deposited in The Arena were now opened, and Judge Rutherford instructed the children how to come and each get a copy thereof, those in the rear half of The Arena marching in two columns out through a side exit, and those in the front half of The Arena marching up over the platform and out through a rear exit. As the march began, the orchestra (minus all its children instrumentalists) struck up and rendered songs, "Children of the Heavenly King," "The Sword of the Lord and of Gideon," and "Who Is on the Lord's Side?" while the vast audience sang. Never was there a more moving sight in these "last days". Many, including strong men, wept at the demonstration. Receiving the gift, the marching children clasped it to them, not a toy or plaything for idle pleasure, but the Lord's provided instrument for most effective work in the remaining months before Armageddon. What a gift! and to so many! The manner of releasing the new book *Children* was an outright surprise to all, but the almighty hand of the All-wise One, Jehovah, was in it, and the maneuver was most blessed indeed. Thereafter *Children*, the author's edition, was disposed of to adult conventioners, on a contribution.

The blessings of the Assembly were further enhanced by the afternoon session, which provided a delightful anticlimax to "Children's Day". The Arena was again packed out to hear about "Your New Work" and the president's parting words. For weeks the question had been upon many consecrated minds, and at 3 p.m. the first speaker, the factory and office servant at Brooklyn, disclosed the "new work", to wit, the placing of *Children*, and thereafter, over a period of three weeks, sending each obtainer, at no extra cost to him, the "*Children* Study Course", to wit, three attractive, illuminated question-and-answer folders, these to be followed the fourth week by a back-call service by the one placing *Children*. Another speaker, on "Solving the Problem", showed how the new book, together with the "*Children* Study Course", provided the solution for the problem of company publishers to reach their individual quota of twelve back-calls monthly and one model study weekly, as suggested in the recent communication of the president of the Society. Three speakers then spoke, each briefly on "When to Begin", and were in concert as to the answer, that NOW is the time.

## Figure 2

The excerpt above is from the left column of p. 288 of the September 15, 1941, *Watchtower*. It is obvious that the "prophet" failed again, for it is stated that the book *Children* was to be "the Lord's provided instrument for most effective work in the *remaining months before Armageddon*" (italics added).

17

to the door are sincere in their methods, but they are deceived by the Watchtower Society, just as I was. After I was finished with *Let God Be True*, I was invited to go with them to see how witnessing was done. I found it interesting and a few years later tried going by myself.

By 1948 we began attending more meetings as a family. My husband, who had shown some interest, became more involved, and two years later when he was invited to go with one of the Witness men in the door-to-door visitation, he went. He found it easy to place literature, and from then on we both became very active, rarely missing any meetings. We also began going out every Sunday morning to do door-to-door witnessing. In addition, I went out on a weekday with some of the women, doing what was called mid-week witnessing; I also began conducting "Bible studies" with interested people. In 1951 I was baptized at a circuit assembly held in McKeesport, Pennsylvania. My husband was baptized later at the international convention in New York City in 1953.

One of the things that bothered me was that the Society didn't contribute to charities except among their own people. I thought this was wrong, but was told that our job was to preach the gospel and that the world should take care of charities. I didn't like this explanation, but thinking that no organization was perfect, I let it go at that. As the years went by, I began to notice that the interpretation of certain scriptures was changed. I objected to this also, but was told that the new understanding was "new light," and they quoted Proverbs 4:18: "But the path of the just is as the shining light, that shineth more and more unto the perfect day." This didn't satisfy me, as I thought of II Timothy 3:7: "Ever learning, and never able to come to the knowledge of the truth." I know now that Proverbs 4:18 was misinterpreted by the Witnesses. The entire fourth chapter of Proverbs must be read to under-

18

stand verse 18. The chapter is an exhortation to find wisdom and avoid wickedness.

At this time I found out that as long as a person was only studying with Jehovah's Witnesses, it was all right to disagree on certain issues or scriptures, but once he became a Witness, he was told that he could not question the Society or express his viewpoint at all. In fact, at an assembly one year, the circuit servant made the statement that if we questioned any decisions made by the Society, we were questioning God. At this time I began to have serious doubts in my heart and mind, and I realize now that the Holy Spirit was dealing with me to come out of a system that was setting itself up as God. My husband and I discussed this and he felt the same way. I also know that I should have come out of this group then. I must have grieved the Holy Spirit by staying a few more years. Since we had become so deeply enmeshed, I didn't want to believe that the Witnesses were wrong. However, we began to attend meetings less regularly and to do our field service less frequently.

Often the lessons in *The Watchtower* were completely about the organization. In these lessons nothing was written about Christ—only how wonderful the organization was. Part of one lesson was about people who were leaving the organization, and one thought stood out prominently: any person who left was turning his back on God. To me, this was blasphemy, and I thought, "Oh, they really were calling the organization God." Further on, the lesson related how these people would never have a chance to live in the new world because they would be destroyed by God at Armegeddon, for only those within the organization would be saved. I believe that there were many discontented Witnesses who were frightened by this lesson into staying in the movement, but this was the main reason for our leaving. I remembered many articles written by the Society that ridiculed Roman Catholics who stayed with a church which threatened them with hell if they left. In that same year another article by the Society exhorted Jehovah's Witnesses not to read anyone else's religious literature because this would be disloyal to Jehovah. What colossal nerve! At our service meetings, we had demonstrations periodically to show us how to handle people who told us they were not allowed to read our literature. We were instructed to say: "You are a free moral agent and no organization has the right to tell you what to read or what not to read. This is for you to decide." Other similar statements were employed.

Our children had already quit going to meetings. Our son was working, and our daughter away at college didn't search out a Kingdom Hall there. However, because they had always been obedient, they went to the meetings with us while they were under our authority. I realize now that we should have left as soon as we began to suspect that this was not God's organization. I stopped going out in the witness work and missed most of the meetings; my husband had already stopped going. I was wondering how I would go about leaving—should I go and speak to the overseer, or just leave and say nothing?

A short time later the Society changed the meaning of a Bible passage for the second time (Rom. 13:1, 2). This was the final straw! I walked out of the Kingdom Hall in the fall of 1962, knowing that I would never go back again.

It was then that I started searching through the back issues of *The Watchtower*. I found many more discrepancies, contradictions, and changes of interpretation. One of these was a short-lived misinterpretation of the Lord's supper (Lord's evening meal). It was in *The Watchtower* of March 15, 1954:

". . . he said: 'Take, eat. This means my body.' " . . .
To which body was Jesus referring here? To his fleshly

20

body? Hardly, for concerning it we read that not a bone was broken, whereas Jesus broke the loaf. (John 19:36) Rather, he was referring to his spiritual body, the Christian congregation. . . [p. 174].

(This interpretation was changed in *The Watchtower* of January 15, 1956, p. 49.) True theology does not need correction! After I looked through the publications and found other similar problems, I set them aside and began studying the Bible without literature aids of any kind. I read chapter by chapter, looking up cross references whenever necessary. The Holy Spirit revealed many things to me, and I was amazed to find that orthodox Christianity was really true. I discovered that the Bible taught such doctrines as: the Trinity, the deity of Christ, the personality of the Holy Spirit, the immortality of the soul, and the visible return of Christ—*all* the doctrines the Watchtower Society had brainwashed us into rejecting! But the most wonderful discovery that my husband and I made came in 1964, when we met our Lord and Savior in the pages of the Bible. Yes, Christ is our God! The Jehovah of the Old Testament is the Christ of the New! I know now that the Witnesses' difficulty is that they are blinded to the truth of the Bible's teaching concerning Christ. Through our honest study of the Bible we also found that salvation is not in an organization, denomination, a creed, or in anything else. Salvation is in a Person, and that Person is Christ! The "narrow way" spoken of in Matthew 7:14 is the Jesus way, as He Himself states in John 14:6. The Bible teaches that nothing can be added to the blood of Christ for salvation (I Pet. 1:18, 19). The whole theme of the Bible from Genesis to Revelation is Christ. Because Witnesses do not understand the Trinity, they feel that it cannot be true. They do not realize that finite men cannot totally understand the infinite. Christ is the one Channel whereby men are saved. The true Church of God is made up

21

of all "born again" believers (John 3:3) from all over the world, regardless of affiliation, kindred, or tongue (John 3:16). However, I feel true Christians will seek a church where the Bible is honored and Christ is preached.

The Jehovah's Witnesses who were my best friends knew that we had left for doctrinal reasons, but they kept urging us to return. Sometimes, when they were out in the service, they would drop in. One of them phoned me one day and said that even if I had made a mistake by leaving, I should come back because the Society directs all the Christian work here on earth. I replied that Jesus Christ directs His work on earth. When I said this, she hung up without even saying good-bye.

One night, as I was thinking about what we should do now that we had found Christ, I turned on the radio and heard a minister preaching a sermon on "The Assurance of Salvation." I told my husband we should visit a Bible-believing church as soon as we could. We visited the church of the minister I had heard and liked it very much except that it was too far from our home. We visited several other conservative churches and finally decided on one about eight miles away. To our amazement we found that all conservative ministers preached the same basic doctrines, even if they represented different denominations and had gone to different theological schools.

One Sunday, a Jehovah's Witness whom we hadn't seen for a long time, brought the new congregation leader to our home. He was the son-in-law of the previous overseer. He was very arrogant when we told him that we would never go back to the group and that he had no jurisdiction over us because we were no longer Jehovah's Witnesses. I pointed out that according to their own literature, those who are not active with the organization are not Jehovah's Witnesses. I also told him, "We preach only Christ now." After I had made that statement twice, he became angry and said, "Christ is dead!" I quoted

22

Hebrews 13:8: "Jesus Christ the same yesterday, and today, and forever." He realized that he had said the wrong thing—the surprise was registered in the face of the other Witness. Before the overseer left, I told him he was very immature and arrogant. We didn't see him again until almost four years later.

Late in 1968 I met at a shopping center a Jehovah's Witness whom I hadn't seen since we had left the organization in 1962. She asked me why I had left. Here I saw the opportunity to tell her how the Society had changed its doctrines and perverted the Bible. I also told her that the organization was taking the place of God and that a changing theology was a false one. She obviously did not like what I had said, and she probably told her husband about it. They both were close friends of the overseer and his father-in-law. Just a few weeks later the overseer came to the house with a member of the congregation committee. I knew this visit was a result of my conversation with the Witness at the shopping center. He said that he had come back to see if we were planning to return to the Kingdom Hall or not. I had to remind him of what we had told him years before. We also indicated that we had been going to church, and as long as we had religious freedom in America, we would go where we pleased. That didn't seem to matter at this point because he said that if we wouldn't come back, he would take action against us. The next Sunday the committee member came back with another member of the committee. They again wanted to know if we would come back. They also warned us that they would take action if we did not return. After a brief conversation they departed. We never got an official letter from the Society, but apparently an announcement about our case was made in the Kingdom Hall, because after that, most Witnesses would not even say hello to us when we met in public places. One Sunday, when I was on the front porch, a Witness who had been a good friend passed our house while she was out in the service. I called her by name and said hello. She looked at me briefly and immediately turned her head away. Some time later my husband went for income tax service to an office where the worker happened to be a Witness. She said, "I'm not allowed to talk to you." She did, however, fill out his form. Another instance occurred in a store where I met a Witness who had been a good friend. I went up to him and said hello and addressed him by name. He looked at me in dismay and said, "Oh! I'm not allowed to talk with you!" I couldn't understand a big, strapping man in his fifties making a frightened statement like that. I replied, "I'm so sorry that you are under such bondage. I am allowed to talk to all my friends. I will pray for you."

I feel sorry for these people who are so regimented that they are fearful about even greeting old friends who left the organization. These are the very people who would ridicule Catholics for being under the domination of their priests. I recalled how friendly and warm our Methodist friends had been whenever we met. They didn't refuse to talk to us because we had left the Methodist church.

Since finding the freedom and salvation that is in Christ, we have been blessed in many ways; God has answered many of my prayers, and I have faith that some of my old friends will come out of the bondage that I once was under.

**Kenneth and Monique Guindon**

# IV

## TWICE ENSLAVED—
## FREE IN CHRIST!

by

Kenneth Guindon

"My sheep listen to my voice, and I know them, and they follow me" (John 10:27 NWT).

I was sixteen years old when I came into contact with the Jehovah's Witnesses and I exchanged one form of slavery for another. I didn't know the meaning of John 10:27 or of Paul's words in Galatians 5:1: "For such freedom Christ set us free. Therefore stand fast, and do not let yourselves be confined again in a yoke of slavery" (NWT).

My friend's mother was a Witness and during one of my visits to his home I noticed the Witnesses' publications in the magazine rack. I was a Catholic at the time, and an article about the Virgin Mary interested me. My friend's mother lost no time in witnessing to me about Jehovah, Armageddon, and man's hope to live through the coming end of the world

25

into a paradise earth. This was really exciting news to me, but believing the Catholic "system" to be the right religion I set about to show her she was wrong in her beliefs. She told me that Jesus wasn't God, that there was no Trinity, and that hell wasn't a place of torment. I accepted a Catholic Bible from her and began searching through it for scriptural arguments for my beliefs. This was in 1957.

I was already falling into the web of the Witnesses' attempts to find and trap new victims. I had been approached and had received literature (step 1), and I was ready for the back-call or return visit (step 2), which is their method of watering the seed planted. I responded to the watering like a desert flower after a drought, and our discussions blossomed into a Bible study (step 3). We got together weekly for the study, using *Let God Be True* and the Bible for source material. I was ill-equipped to refute the well-thought-out arguments and interpretive subtleties. I thought that I was really growing in Bible knowledge. I had never before read the Bible, although I had spent six years in a Catholic school. Little did I realize that I was being ensnared in a system of doctrines that would change my whole life, my whole way of thinking, and lead me to be a missionary in Africa for the Watchtower Bible and Tract Society.

As the study progressed I was told about the persecution of true Christians during the first century and was warned that I too would have to expect opposition because Satan was going to be very angry that I was learning "the truth." Already, my mind was being conditioned to resist the objections of my parents, who would soon become aware that I was studying the Bible with the Jehovah's Witnesses and that I was taking the study seriously. I was warned that "a man's enemies will be the persons of his own household" (Matt. 10:34-37 NWT) and that I should be prepared to take up my cross (or "torture

26

Ken Guindon at work in the Brooklyn printing plant

View of the Watchtower Society's Brooklyn printing plant

stake" NWT) and follow him. This is exactly what happened. Nobody patted me on the back to tell me that I was doing well in studying the Bible, but instead my family and friends laughed or scorned, and discouraged me from studying with the Witnesses.

My father said I was "brainwashed." He refused to allow Witness publications in the house, but by then I had been studying for about six months and was well prepared for these attempts by "Satan" to persecute me and make me stop studying the Bible. I had been attending a Tuesday evening Bible study with Jehovah's Witnesses in the neighborhood, where I was welcomed into a little group of about ten to fifteen people, a few of whom I had already met (step 4). By this time I was being invited to attend the Witness meetings at the local Kingdom Hall in Venice, California (step 5).

I was surprised to find that at the Kingdom Hall there was no feeling of worship or that "I had been to church." It was a question-and-answer study where people raised their hands to give or read their answers to the questions found in *The Watchtower* magazine. The average Jehovah's Witness has a good general knowledge of the Bible since he attends five hours of similar group meetings weekly. Another result of this "group therapy" is the thorough "brainwashing" of the individual. One learns to be organization-minded, or as they call it, "theocratic," submissive. Unity above all else! The constant repetition is what explains the uniformity that exists in the Witness meetings; in addition, all their decisions and beliefs are direct communications from Brooklyn, New York. The rejection of blood transfusion is a good example of this uniformity.

Now I was really beginning to feel the pressure to conform. I was told that all real Christians must preach the "good news," and the best way to do that was to take *The Watchtower* and *Awake!* magazines from door to door and look for people with whom I could study the Bible and then lead into the congregation. I became aware of the training program in the local congregation and someone was assigned to help me. We were told not to worry about what the people might say to us because we were sure to know more about the Bible than they. So, armed with four or five Bible texts, I was led into the "field service" (step 6). Imagine being "enthusiastic" about something you would rather not do, but enthusiastic you must be if you are going to get the magazines and books into the hands of the people. Much of the Witnesses' enthusiasm is a trained reflex, the "art of selling."

I was baptized in April, 1957 (step 7), during my first circuit assembly. The circuit assembly was then a three-day meeting of the local congregations, usually grouping about twelve to fifteen congregations. Here I first heard about going to "serve where the need is great." I became aware of the push of the Society to get publishers (preachers of the "good news") to move out to isolated areas in the United States and elsewhere to help start new congregations, or to build up the weaker rural congregations which lacked sufficient members to cover the surrounding towns and farms with the Witness message.

After some correspondence with the Society's headquarters in Brooklyn I was put in touch with some Witness leaders in Maine, where there was a great need for people to come and help the congregations. After attending the international convention of Jehovah's Witnesses in New York in 1958, I continued on, arriving in northern Maine in August of that year. Having had only a year of training with the congregation in California, and the uplift of the experience of attending the New York Assembly, I felt ready to tackle the new task of serving as a pioneer minister. At eighteen years of age I had left my family, my friends, and my job. I would have to find part-time work to support myself. My opinion is that the Jehovah's Witnesses' organization asks a lot from people, but really gives them very little help in return.

I settled down with the Houlton, Maine, congregation of Jehovah's Witnesses and soon learned what kind of work picking potatoes could be. I picked potatoes that fall for a farmer and often thought back on the easier and better-paying job I had left in California. Yet, I was happy to be with other full-time workers with whom I shared an apartment behind the old wooden Kingdom Hall in Houlton. It was a cold winter and I had the feeling that I would never get warm. We did not have adequate fuel for the house, and much of the little heat we did have escaped through the roof and the sides of the building.

In the spring my savings were gone and I could no longer stay in Houlton because I could not find any part-time work there. So I moved to Caribou, Maine, in April, 1959. I found work with some local farmers there who were Jehovah's Witnesses, and I was appointed to work with the local congregation in the capacity of Ministry School servant, or instructor, and leader of the Tuesday evening Bible study. Later I was appointed to serve as the assistant presiding minister.

These years in Caribou proved to be years of development and growth for me as a Jehovah's Witness. I gave many Bible lectures on Sundays and often went to Canada to speak and to attend conventions. A dear family of Jehovah's Witnesses took me and another boy into their home, and life became more enjoyable for us because we had a good place to stay and many good meals. They were farmers, so we had some guarantee of work, which was the biggest problem for us in that area. I worked particularly in the French-speaking areas of northern Maine, and it was during this time that my knowledge of the

French language grew. This would help me later as a missionary to Africa.

It was during my stay in Caribou that I met a man named Dana who belonged to the Baptist church. We discussed the Scriptures together for an hour, and one thing he said to me I was to remember later in life, and this helped me to see that God was using other people to serve Him if they would let Him. He said, "I believe that no one group or church is the right one, but God is using different people from different churches who are born again and saved and these make up the Church or Body of Christ." In 1972 I found myself pondering this thought.

On March 1, 1963, I was reassigned by the Society to Houlton, Maine, as a special pioneer minister, which would mean that the Society would help with expenses by giving me $50.00 a month if I made the goals of 150 hours preaching and teaching, and fifty back-calls in my assigned territory. I was also appointed to serve as the assistant presiding minister in this congregation where I had first started in 1958 as a regular pioneer. Later in the year I was appointed to serve as the presiding minister. Houlton had one of the largest territories in the state. We would travel about eighty miles one way to Millinocket to distribute magazines and look for interested people. Imagine these trips during snowstorms!

In 1963, during a convention of the Witnesses in New York City which I attended, I answered a call for workers to come and work in the printery and world headquarters of the Watchtower Society in Brooklyn. I filled out an application and returned to Houlton to await an answer. In November of 1963, the call came to report. I went not knowing what kind of job I would receive. I didn't like the move to the city, but my attitude was that I was ready to accept anything the

31

Society would assign me to do. "After all," I thought, "isn't this the Lord's organization?"

Workers at the Brooklyn headquarters receive $14.00 as a monthly allowance, and their jobs may vary from working on a large printing press valued at over $400,000, to working in the laundry pressing shirts or in the offices typing letters. All is done in good humor and with a desire to serve and help the brothers throughout the world and to further the advancement of the "kingdom interests" here on the earth. This unselfish desire, brotherly love, and hard work explain the Witnesses' success and some reasons why many are drawn to them.

I lived at Bethel for five years and was assigned to work with various congregations in the city, mostly in the poorer sections of Brooklyn. I was also appointed to the Society's official speaker's staff and traveled up to 200 miles on the weekends to speak in various congregations. I did this about once a month.

In 1967 my future wife came to New York to attend the Watchtower Bible School of Gilead, which was a five-month training school for pioneer workers who already had two years of service. Monique left for her assignment in the Ivory Coast and I followed a year later.

I arrived in the Ivory Coast in September, 1968, after my graduation from Gilead. I would now receive my room and board and $7.00 a month for personal expenses, in return for which I would fulfill the Society quotas and accept any assignment which they might give me. I was assigned to Bouaké in the savanna region of the interior. For six months I worked every day from door to door through the hottest season of the year, talking to everyone I met about the Bible and the Witness message. I already was fluent in French, the official language of the country, but found that many of the people in the district where I worked were of the Moslem religion and they

32

Ken Guindon (right) and a Witness friend with the Bethel Home in the background

Ken and Monique Guindon (left) and two other Witnesses on the porch of the missionary home, Gagnoa, Ivory Coast

spoke the Dioula language. Much of my time was spent approaching women who could not speak French and I felt that these efforts were really fruitless.

In May, 1969, I contracted polio and was hospitalized at Hôpital Central in Bouaké. I remained there for six weeks before I was sent to a special center for polio victims in Paris, France. At first I was quite worried about how I was going to pay for the hospital and medicines because our medical expenses were not guaranteed. I was on the point of death since the polio was quite high in my body. There wasn't an iron lung for adults in the country, so we were worried that the lungs would be touched by the paralysis. It stopped just at the diaphragm. As missionaries we had received vaccinations against yellow fever and smallpox before leaving the States, but we were not vaccinated against polio.

I spent six months hospitalized in Paris and six months as an outpatient. The Watchtower Society paid all of my expenses and boarded me at the Paris branch of the Society. I was shown much kindness and love by the Witnesses in France, and I was strengthened to believe that these were truly God's people on earth. For a time the big question was whether I would ever walk again. Yet, in time I learned to walk and in one year I returned to the Ivory Coast finally to marry the girl I had first loved and waited for in 1967. We were married in May, 1970.

My left leg remained quite weak and from time to time I would fall, but I kept up in the door-to-door ministry. I was given some office work for the Society in Abidjan and my wife was a big help to me, giving me treatments for my muscles. I was no longer able to be the strong, independent person that I once was; now my wife carried the groceries for me. I was given the responsibility for several missionary homes, which meant that I did the paper work and the necessary errands

34

**WATCHTOWER**

BIBLE AND TRACT SOCIETY
OF NEW YORK, INC.

117 ADAMS STREET, BROOKLYN, NEW YORK 11201, U.S.A.

F:FDG                    December 23, 1971

TO WHOM IT MAY CONCERN

    Kenneth R. Guindon served as a full-time field representative of our Society from September 1, 1957, to December 1, 1963. He was then transferred to Brooklyn, New York, to our headquarters of our organization where he served from December 1, 1963, to April 22, 1968, at which time he then went through our Gilead missionary school five and a half month course and then entered into the missionary activity.

    During his time at the Brooklyn headquarters from December 1, 1963, to April 22, 1968, he worked on paper cutters and job presses in our job printing department. Because of his good ability, he was promoted to be supervisor of our handbindery department which he handled for three years before leaving. Additionally, he handled French translation and correspondence received in our office. He performed each of his assignments fully satisfactorily.

    In addition to the above he served as an assistant to the supervising minister in one of our New York congregations as well as addressing congregations in the vicinity of New York City on weekends as a special representative of our Society.

    Our organization has found Mr. Guindon to be very capable and always reliable. In all of his dealings with our Society he was fully honest and trustworthy. He had an excellent attendance record and was of high moral standing. In view of these qualifications, he has our highest recommendation.

Watchtown B. & S. Society
OF NEW YORK, INC.

M. H. Larson, Manager

connected with maintaining a home of from four to twelve people. In Gagnoa, our last assignment, there were four of us in the missionary home: my wife and I and two German missionary girls. I organized all of the meetings and the work in the town we were then just opening up.

When my wife became pregnant in October, 1971, we realized that we would have to take up a new life because the Watchtower Society does not permit children in missionary homes. Missionaries who have children must leave the missionary home and look for a job to support themselves if they wish to remain in that foreign country. So for various reasons, mainly my lack of employment, we returned to the United States.

\* \* \* \* \*

"No man can come to me unless the Father, who sent me, draws him . . ." (John 6:44 NWT).

As we continued to attend the meetings each week, we began to feel the pressure of the Watchtower "system" (Matt. 23:4). We looked to the meetings to build us up, but found that the Tuesday night Bible study dealt with material in the Bible books of Ezekiel and Zechariah and that the organization claimed to be able now to give us light on all of these most difficult passages. We frankly felt that Society interpretations should be open to at least some questioning. Hadn't they changed many points of interpretation in the past? How could they be so dogmatic in saying that these things which occurred in Israel in the past were having modern fulfillment in the Witness organization and in giving precise dates, such as: 1914, 1918, 1925, 1935, and 1939? Would the "end of the world" really come in 1974 or 1975? The Watchtower Society was leading people to think so, and they were planning their lives as though it would. Witnesses were quitting their jobs or working part-time in order to become pioneers. What need would they have for Social Security, or money in the bank, or life insurance, or any of the necessary precautions that people normally take in order to provide for their families?

We observed from our new non-Witness friends and acquaintances, at work and where we lived, that some of them demonstrated a real faith in God and were good-living people. Was God going to destroy them at Armageddon? Did they or did they not have a relationship with Jesus Christ? Could we be judges of such a personal thing?

As I laid aside *The Watchtower* and other study guides of the Jehovah's Witnesses and read the New Testament with an open mind, I became aware of two things. First, salvation comes by faith in Jesus Christ and not by works (Eph. 2:8-10). The believer has eternal life when he believes in the Son of God (I John 5:1-13). Second, we all have as a result one hope, *not two*. Ephesians 4:4 shows this, but the Witnesses really believe in two hopes for Christians. The Witnesses say only 144,000 are born again (Rev. 14:1), and that the rest of mankind will live on the earth; they call them "other sheep" (John 10:16). I now realize that this was man's system and that there is but one faith and one hope—the faith that is in Christ Jesus and the hope that is everlasting life. Why should I let men take away what the New Testament offers?

Now, without trying do disprove the Witnesses' teaching or trying to find reasons to leave them, I kept on reading the Scriptures to find out if they really did teach that Jesus Christ, the Son of God, was really God. I read books about other religions and books by ex-Witnesses and opened my mind to ideas and facts. At the meetings I examined the spirituality and seriousness of other Witnesses and the content of what was being said there. Did they really hold up Jesus to the extent the Bible does? I found out that they said one thing but believed another. They will often speak highly of Jesus' sacrifice and yet deny its efficacy by saying that to be saved one must do all the things the organization directs.

I went to several church services with some of my friends, and there I saw love and respect for Jesus Christ and heard the call to come to Him and accept Him as my personal Lord and Savior. I wanted to answer that call, but refrained, having made up my mind to decide not emotionally but logically by what I saw doctrinally in the Scriptures. Two books helped me immensely, *The Kingdom of the Cults* and *The Jehovah's Witnesses and Prophetic Speculation.* I really feel it was of the Lord to have been able by His grace and power to overthrow in my mind the domination of the Jehovah's Witnesses. The Lord provided the right friends, the right books, and the right churches.

On March 16, 1973, we sent our letter of resignation to the Witnesses. My wife, who had been a Witness since she was twelve, has been led by the Lord's Spirit to understand the meaning of I Corinthians 12:3. We accept that the Lord Jesus is *Jehovah.* What a mystery, but what a revelation! We have been baptized by evangelicals in water, in symbol of our death, burial, and resurrection with Christ and our dedication to Him. We invite all sincere people, especially Jehovah's Witnesses, to lay aside the Watchtower interpretations and accept God's Word simply as it reads. This is the only way to enjoy peace with God through Jesus. Jesus tells us: "Come to me, all whose work is hard, whose load is heavy; and I will give you relief" (Matt. 11:28 NEB). Do you believe Jesus' words or do you want to follow men?

**Douglas and Barbara Wiskow**

V

**WE LEFT "the truth"
FOR THE TRUTH**

by

Douglas Wiskow

I have written this testimony not so much to show my negative reaction to the Watchtower Bible and Tract Society but to record my positive response to Jesus Christ. My hope is that my experience will be of benefit to someone in search of the truth.

In 1959, at the age of 15, I left organized Christianity feeling that it had nothing to offer me in my search for the meaning of life. Organized religion, as I saw it, was guilty of the charges later related to me by the Jehovah's Witnesses. Hypocrisy, complacency, and inactivity abounded, and many religious organizations supported governments with long histories of bloody wars and other inhumanities. In my personal religious activities I had no relationship with Jesus Christ and felt that "the church," because of its failures in other areas,

39

was not the vehicle that would lead me into a meaningful relationship with God.

For the next eleven years I sought truth and "God" along many avenues. I dabbled in politics, social causes, drugs, Eastern religion, philosophy, and humanistic psychology. If it claimed to be the path to reality and truth, I tried it. For all my sincere and conscientious investigation I was still left empty. None of these disciplines or escape mechanisms filled the void, the need within me. I doubted whether God existed. And I was sure that salvation (whatever that was!) was something internal that I had to work out for myself. I felt all that was necessary to find happiness was to educate myself properly. Even if I didn't know all the answers, someone did. All I had to do was find him.

At this stage of my life I was really confused. I had no God, no hope, no security. My wife Barbara, whom I had married in 1968, was a practicing Catholic at the time and had been urging me to attend church with her and to study the Bible with a priest. I refused, and after a while my criticism of Catholicism began to take its toll on her. She wanted to understand the Bible and to bring me to God, but became frustrated in her attempts to do so as a Catholic. Then one day in the summer of 1970 one of Jehovah's Witnesses came to our door and I was willing to listen to the views of this group. Soon we agreed to a Bible study with this impartial (in terms of my wife's Catholicism and my agnosticism) third party who represented an organization that held some of the same political and social views we did.

Thus began our association with the Watchtower Bible and Tract Society and the organization of Jehovah's Witnesses. The conduct of the Witnesses was exemplary, they were neatly and modestly dressed, and their children were well behaved and obedient. They all appeared to have a special warm and friendly association among themselves, addressing everyone as "brother" or "sister." In retrospect, I can understand how easily we were attracted by this organization that claimed to be the *only* organization on earth guided by God's "holy spirit," and the *only* organization capable of understanding the meaning of the Holy Scriptures (*The Watchtower*, July 1, 1973, p. 402).

In the course of our three years with the organization we were taught doctrines and "truths" from Watchtower publications in a clear and logical manner. When questions arose, other Watchtower publications were cited as references because it was claimed that the Watchtower Bible and Tract Society was God's "sole collective channel for the flow of Biblical truth to men on earth" in these last days (*The Watchtower*, July 15, 1960, p. 439). We were taught that we must adhere absolutely to the decisions and scriptural understandings of the Society because God had given it this authority over his people (*The Watchtower*, May 1, 1972, p. 272). Therefore, because I wanted to gain eternal life, I accepted and preached everything I was told, even if I didn't always fully understand or believe it.

To gain this eternal life, I was told, certain things were necessary: 1) I should study the Bible diligently, and only through Watchtower publications. 2) I should attend all five meetings each week. 3) I should devote as many hours as possible to the ministry work. 4) I should associate only with other Jehovah's Witnesses. 5) I should be baptized. (I was baptized on July 20, 1973, at Dodger Stadium.) All of these things, and more, must accompany faith, because earning the reward of *eternal life requires hard work* (*The Watchtower*, August 15, 1972, pp. 491-497). Even faith was expressed in terms of work (i.e., "exercises faith," John 11:26 NWT).

After three years of association with the Jehovah's Witnesses, through the efforts of my wife's parents we came in contact with the ministries of two "born again" Christians, former Jehovah's Witnesses (Edmond Gruss and Kenneth Guindon). Through Mr. Gruss's publications and discussions with Mr. Guindon I took to heart two beliefs that changed my life.

First, the Watchtower Bible and Tract Society is not God's channel of truth. To come to this conclusion one need only look at the errors and contradictions in the doctrinal and prophetic understanding of the Society over the years. In addition, because they have spoken prophetically in the name of Jehovah (YHWH), and what they have said has failed to occur, the Watchtower Bible and Tract Society is a false prophet by the definition of Deuteronomy 18:20-22.[1]

Second, in contradiction to the teachings of the Watchtower Bible and Tract Society, I believe that salvation is the free gift of God granted to anyone who accepts Jesus Christ as his Lord and personal Savior, exclusive of any and all works (Rom. 3:21, 24; John 3:14-18). Salvation is not found in any organization, it is in Jesus Christ (Acts 4:12).

On Thursday, October 18, 1973, I accepted Jesus Christ as my Lord and Savior and was saved (Acts 16:30-31). The next day my wife asked Jesus to come into her life, and from that point on we have been free in Christ (Gal. 5:1). I brought my confusion, my fears, my problems, my failures, and my shortcomings to Jesus and asked him to take over in my life. It is a real blessing to enjoy the satisfying inner peace that comes from knowing and trusting in the promises of our Lord (Matt. 11:28-30). He died for *all* of my sins—yesterday, today, and forever! He paid my debt in full and for this I

---

1. See Edmond C. Gruss, *The Jehovah's Witnesses and Prophetic Speculation* (Nutley, N. J.: Presbyterian and Reformed Publishing Co., 1972), chap. 3, which deals with the Witnesses' position on the 1914 second coming of Christ.

can't help loving Him (John 1:29). On October 25, 1973, I wrote the following letter to the Carpinteria congregation of Jehovah's Witnesses removing my spiritual fellowship from that organization. I love these people and will miss them very much. They are exceedingly zealous and very sincere, but I also feel they are tragically deceived.

If you are a Jehovah's Witness I pray that this testimony will cause you to examine your beliefs today—right now! Jesus is standing at the door of your heart asking to come in (Rev. 3:20). He offers you the *gift* of eternal life, and all you need to do is accept it. There are no strings attached. There is nothing else you must do; in fact, there is nothing else you can do! Salvation is not a reward—it is a gift (Rom. 6:23). I know I have eternal life now, as a present possession (I John 5:11-13). Pray that Jehovah, through the power of the Holy Spirit, might lead you to the real Truth—our Lord and Savior Jesus Christ (John 14:6).

October 25, 1973

Dear Friends,

It is after much prayerful study and thought that I am making public my decision to remove myself from the Carpinteria congregation of Jehovah's Witnesses as well as from association with the Watchtower Bible and Tract Society of Pennsylvania. I have not associated myself with any other religious group or organization. Rather, my decision is based on my personal conviction that certain of the beliefs and teachings of the Society are in conflict with both the Holy Scriptures and human evidence.

I look around and I see too many good people who love God and accept Jesus as the savior of mankind, and are not Jehovah's Witnesses, to believe that salvation will come only to those who are part of this organization. The Bible tells us that eternal life is gained through faith in Jesus Christ, not faithful service in *any* organization. (John 3:15-17) I truly believe Paul's claim that we are saved by the undeserved kindness of God through our faith in Jesus Christ; and that good works are the result of salvation, not the cause of it. (Ephesians 2:8-10)

I do not believe that "Jehovah's organization" alone is capable of understanding the Holy Scriptures. (See "Praise Jehovah With His People," *Watchtower*, July 1, 1973, p. 402) Nor do I accept all of the positions taken by the Society on prophetic and doctrinal understanding of the Bible. Considering the changes in doctrinal matters and the errors in prophetic speculation over the years, it is difficult, if not impossible to believe that this organization is the sole recipient of, or is guided at all by God's Holy Spirit. In light of these errors and changes, I find I cannot trust this organization to decide doctrine or interpret prophecy for me. By their own admission the Watchtower Bible and Tract Society has been wrong before. How do I know they are not wrong now?

We love you all very much and will miss associating with you (I assume my actions will result in my being disfellowshiped), but it is our firm conviction that Jehovah's Witnesses are misguided in their search for truth and salvation. My wife and I will no longer be attending meetings and are at this time withdrawing our spiritual fellowship from the organization of Jehovah's Witnesses.

Sincerely,

Douglas W. Wiskow

**Donald and Evelyn Bedwell**

VI

## LED BY THE LORD INTO THE LIGHT

by

Evelyn Bedwell

I am very thankful to be able to share with others just a few of the many ways in which the Lord has led in our lives. My husband and I feel that we have been especially blessed, for God not only brought us out of an organization from which few escape, but He also guided us every step of the way, back into fellowship with Christ.

From the time I was a child of nine I had faith in Christ and fellowship in prayer with the Lord, but my formal training in the Bible or in church was almost nonexistent. I learned most of what I knew from my godly grandmother and great-grandmother.

As a young bride I joined my husband's church (Methodist) in Chester, Pennsylvania. A few years later, after his dis-

45

charge from the army, we settled in my home town, Martinsburg, West Virginia. We transferred our membership to a Presbyterian church, where we were active in all phases of the work.

Even as far back as 1943, when I was a young married woman in Chester, a Jehovah's Witness woman studied with me intermittently for several years. At that time it was only an interesting pastime for a lonely girl in a strange city.

For years, even while active in church, I was a babe-in-Christ and never got beyond a spiritual milk diet. I had always wanted to know and understand more about God's Word, but I just didn't feel that I was able to study and understand the Bible myself. I didn't realize that God's Holy Spirit would have guided me; instead I thought I must turn to some man or religion with superior understanding or insight. I had a great many unanswered questions and felt a need to know God's Word in greater depth.

In the fall of 1950, a Jehovah's Witness couple called on us, and they seemed to have all the answers. They came every week and studied with us, giving of their time and of themselves to be there. They "proved" their false doctrine by quoting Bible verses, but I know now that these were twisted and out of context. Their study material came from publications of the Watchtower Society and was the reasoning of man. They continually stressed that the Watchtower Bible and Tract Society was "God's only channel of communication on earth today" and pointed out the shortcomings of the rest of the world, and of Christendom in particular. These statements were repeated over and over as fact, until they became truth to our deluded minds. We were slowly and methodically brainwashed and indoctrinated.

The zealous activity of the Witnesses impressed us. They went out and ministered to people from door to door instead of

46

waiting for them to come to church. They also had a completely organized training program.

Once converts have been carefully trained as Witnesses, they accept almost anything the Society says. They believe they are God's people and the only ones to whom the Holy Spirit gives understanding of the Bible, an understanding which is supposed to be from Jehovah and cannot be doubted on the smallest point; yet, it constantly changes. (How can an unchanging God change His mind about truths that have been taught dogmatically as from Him?) These revisions are called "new light" or "meat in due season." Once the Witnesses get in this frame of mind, the Society becomes their God, for all information is supposed to be from God through the "Faithful and discreet slave class" who dispenses information through the Watchtower publications. Jehovah's Witnesses turn to the organization as Christians turn to Christ. It becomes their savior, because remaining in the organization is the only hope of salvation. At this stage they receive information just like an unthinking computer. Watchtower brainwashing is a deceptive, hypnotic process.

The Christ of the Jehovah's Witnesses is different from the biblical Christ. He isn't a personal Savior but an organizational savior. They will concede that he is the Son of God, but it is thought to be blasphemous to say that He is God. He is only the archangel Michael to them. There are two classes in the Jehovah's Witnesses. One claims to be the 144,000 of Revelation who alone are Christ's spiritual brothers, the anointed, the only ones called to go to heaven, if they don't fall away before death. The other class contains the average Witnesses, called "Jonadabs," who look forward to eternal life on a paradise earth. These, who never dare take communion, do not even claim salvation through Christ's atonement, but might be saved if they serve Christ's brothers, the anointed.

47

They ultimately will stand before God "on the basis of their own righteousness." (Read pp. 391, 392 of *Life Everlasting— in Freedom of the Sons of God.*)

* * * * *

My husband was baptized into the organization in the summer of 1952 and I in September, 1953. Later, as a young teen, our older son was also baptized. We all became robot-like slaves for the Watchtower Bible and Tract Society. It is a religion which requires total submission.

I could never describe the full extent of my misery and confusion all those years I was in the organization. I felt hurt and was secretly resentful toward the Lord because I had lost fellowship with Him. When I prayed, I felt as though the Watchtower Society was a great barrier. For God to be so distant seemed unfair, since I knew more and worked harder for salvation than I ever had before. Why would He desert me now? What could be wrong with me? The Lord dealt with me continually, but I thought it must be Satan putting these doubts in my mind and only turned closer to the organization. I was handicapped with arthritis and couldn't do what I thought I should. I felt guilty when I wasn't out in the door-to-door work, and guilty, frustrated, and useless when I was. There was a never-ending battle within me. My heart told me that something was wrong, while my head told me that I had studied and knew I was right. I didn't dare mention to fellow Witnesses that once I thought I was saved, for such a view was considered by the Witnesses as egotistical and blasphemous, because it was taking the judgment from God.

Much of the fruitage I saw among the Witnesses was bad. There seemed to be more than an average amount of immorality, insanity, gossip, hatred, jealousy, lying, broken homes—I could go on and on. I couldn't understand this. It didn't add up. I determined that we were being attacked by Satan because we

48

were God's organization. There were very few Witnesses with whom I was able to become friends. I didn't like them, and I didn't even care too much for myself. I didn't realize that with Christ all things are possible but of ourselves we can do nothing (Phil. 4:13; John 15:5).

I took my unhappiness out on my loved ones. We were a picky, quarrelsome, fanatically driven family. Our older son was never allowed to be a normal child. When he wasn't in school, he was out in service, at meetings, or at studies. We picked at, pushed, and criticized this child that God had given us, and allowed others in the organization to do the same, until he had a nervous breakdown when he was fifteen. Just this alone shows me that in spite of all my good morals and works, without the grace and mercy of God, I would bear the responsibility of parental failure. The only reason our other son was spared such an experience was that he was ten years younger. The Lord has forgiven me for mistreating my older son, but I doubt that I can ever forgive myself.

On May 30, about seven years ago, a friend and I were out in the magazine work. She called on Pastor Dell, the pastor of Rosemont Grace Brethren Church, where we are now members. I stopped by later to see what had detained her. I could say that it was coincidence, but I believe that it was by the hand of God, that Ted Dencher, a former Witness, was there. He had been speaking at the church. He sent my friend one of his books and she and her husband read it, but she felt that she shouldn't keep it. It came into my possession through my son. I knew enough about the organization by this time that I believed Mr. Dencher's testimony, but I felt that he could change his doctrines only out of bitterness or revenge. I wasn't very impressed, but it planted a seed of doubt, to find out that an active Witness had come free.

Things had already started to happen in our Witness

congregation. My husband had been one of the servants (elders) for many years. During this time there had been occasional disagreements. We were still spiritually sensitive enough to see that things were wrong and that unscriptural things were practiced and condoned. My husband tried to stand up for what was right and to help others. We discounted rumors that the other servants were "out to get" my husband, yet strange things began to happen. For instance, at my mother's death there wasn't a word of sympathy or even a card; we sat alone on viewing evening. Soon my husband was very formally called before the committee for alleged inhospitality. The wife of the assistant overseer claimed she had come to visit and I wouldn't come to the door. She had never visited us in all those years. I was attending a P.T.A. meeting at our son's school at the time and could have proven that I wasn't home. It was just pick and hurt, but we still paid little attention. We knew that such unkindness was in the nature of some of them, but never dreamed that these people with whom we had worked closely for years could be motivated to disfellowship us.

By this time our older son was twenty-one and married to a Witness girl. The overseer still badgered him. Finally, at the request of our son, after the overseer had again publicly humiliated him, my husband tried to talk with him about this. My husband made it clear that if he could do nothing but destroy our children, he should let them alone. The overseer flared up and made accusations. Although my husband was in the right, he graciously went to the overseer's home and tried to patch up the differences, but he would not listen and my husband was deprived of all position and privileges. Later I asked the congregational leaders about this, and the assistant overseer told me that he was "trying to teach that Don Bedwell some humility."

They finally got their way, and my husband was disfellowshiped for "disloyalty to his fellow servants." When they sent for him, they did not even tell him that it was a disfellowshiping hearing. After I learned what kind of meeting it was, I asked if I could be a witness for him. The circuit servant only shoved me and was rude.

At this time I was very humble before the authority of the Society and felt sure that they would follow the published rules. When one is disfellowshiped, he is viewed as dead before God and all Jehovah's Witnesses. He ceases to exist and even his immediate family, if they are not under his roof and care, can have nothing to do with him.

Several friends and I spoke with the circuit servant and told him of the lies and injustice of the hearing. Four of us were called in and told that we could not question the authority of the overseer. I was told that if I felt that the hearing was not just, it was not only my right, but my duty, to write the Society. I could hardly believe some of the things which were stated, and I said, "Do you mean that if the overseer tells me to do something unscriptural, I have to do it?" The spokesman of the committee, with the agreement of those with him, said, "Emphatically yes, if he tells you to do something wrong your blood will be on his hands."

If a church were corrupt, a person could move on to another of his choice, but in the Watchtower Society the local congregation is all that there is and one cannot even attend another. He must attend where he is assigned. As much as I wanted to be free of the harassment of these people, I was bound by their rules.

I wrote a very humble letter asking the Society to look into the matter of my husband's disfellowshiping. Then I also was disfellowshiped, for "attempting to discredit the servants in the Martinsburg Congregation." The assistant overseer laughed

51

at me because they had tricked me into following their advice. I had been so careful to follow the rules because I knew of their intentions to find fault with me, and now in spite of my carefulness, they succeeded. I just wish there were space to go into the unbelievable ugliness and lying of this experience. The rules of the Watchtower Society and even of common decency were all broken. I wasn't allowed any witnesses, and my accusers were also the committee who were my judges (to them, an impartial committee). I was very shocked, not by being disfellowshiped, but by seeing men I had followed for years descend to such depths before my eyes. It was all so groundless and so full of coincidences that I believe with all my heart that God used this means to strike us down and make us see just as surely as he did the apostle Paul (Acts 9).

But all that happened was still not enough to make me leave the Witnesses. For a year and a half I sat at every meeting thinking of myself as a Christian martyr, but had no contact with the members because to them I had ceased to exist. I had always felt sorry for disfellowshiped people, yet I was surprised to find that I felt almost contented for the first time in years. I sometimes wondered if this was the devil working on me, but I didn't really believe that. I think the Lord meant for me to sit there because I was beginning to see the organization for what it really was. I thought, "Could this be the great pearl of wisdom I had trusted with my life?" I was sure of one thing and that was that I didn't want to return.

About five years ago, a terrible thing happened that ultimately drew me closer to Christ. Our older son, who by now had a little son of his own, was working with dynamite and as he bent over it, it blew up in his face. He was in shock and refused treatment for nearly a day. He required over a hundred and fifty stitches, but worst of all, he was blind. He should have been dead; only a rib kept a stone from going into his heart. I was near hysteria and I just could not stand the thought of his being blind and disfigured. Early on Easter morning, in the car in front of the hospital, I prayed as I never had prayed before. It seemed as though I just could not take no as an answer. After a while, a feeling of peace and assurance came over me such as I had never experienced. I again felt fellowship with Christ. Although my son was blind for two weeks, I knew he would be all right. I won't even attempt to explain it, but he was healed. I know only that the Lord did it and gave me assurance that He would. There was nothing the doctor could do but deaden the pain. My son not only has good eyesight now, but doesn't even need the glasses he wore before. Even his scars are small. Two outstanding eye specialists have called him a miracle patient. Three tiny stones had been blown entirely through his eyes, yet his sight is better than before. One doctor said that he had done nothing, that God had done it all. Other doctors were called in to see his eyes because the recovery was so unbelievable. Many times I have asked myself why, after the miraculous healing, my son didn't leave the organization entirely, and accept Christ. Just a few months ago it came to me that this had not been meant for him but was to lead me back to Christ.

I had promised God that if He would heal my son I would do His will as it was revealed to me. I don't know what I could have been thinking, because without even waiting for God's leading, I decided He must want me to apply for reinstatement in the Watchtower Society. I just felt sick over this decision, yet I did all I could to be reinstated. At the hearing, the new overseer, who seemed like a nice young man, said that I was a credit to the congregation. He praised me repeatedly. He said that he could find no fault with me, yet he turned his palms up and shrugged and said, "My hands are tied." He was the final authority on my case. It was just as though the Lord took direct action in several instances. My only explanation now for my not being reinstated is that I prayed, but since I didn't know about waiting on the Lord, I felt I myself must figure it out. I had prayed earnestly for deliverance from this confusion, and the Lord was doing it in spite of all I did to resist and grieve the Holy Spirit.

My husband was reinstated, but couldn't stand it. He finally quit attending meetings and then resigned. I had been studying the Bible some now, but unfortunately it was the Witnesses' biased New World Translation.

Later, when I went to the hospital for a knee operation, I again saw Pastor Dell as he called on another patient. I felt that I just must talk with him, but then I thought how futile such a talk would be because of our different beliefs. I felt a sense of loss and depression when he left.

I was conscious of a new confusion now. Where could I turn? The Witnesses had made me critical and suspicious of churches, and some with which I had been familiar deserved my distrust. I felt as though I didn't belong any place. Surely God didn't intend for me to spend my life in a lonely spiritual vacuum.

The Lord had run me down and backed me into a corner until I finally totally surrendered to Christ. I really had no other choice. I knew nothing except that the Lord would have to guide me because I trusted no man or denomination and the only place I was sure that I would find truth was in the Bible. I didn't even realize that my choice was the one the Lord wanted. The Word of God began to open to me. I prayed and studied for long hours. I suppose I was a bit frantic in my urgency, but I could not stand this confusion any longer. I compared translations, taking each verse and asking myself what it said. I read and reread passages. I prayed for guidance and understanding. It was becoming clear and I had the assurance of the Holy Spirit that orthodox teachings were indeed taught in the Bible.

Then another problem arose. I was ready to associate with a good church, but had strong doubts that such a church existed. What should I do now? Again I asked for the Lord's leading and this time I waited. This was out of desperation. It was all I could do. I surely wasn't going to shop through all those hundreds of churches and cults. I had already wasted too many years searching in all the wrong places.

By this time I did feel competent enough to talk with my husband and share what I had found through my study with a former Witness friend who had been disfellowshiped years before we were.

Just over three years ago a Billy Graham crusade, led by Lane Adams, came to town for two weeks. It seems that it is unusual for a crusade of this size to be held in a town as small as ours. I went with a cynical, suspicious attitude. I especially didn't like this sort of display. In spite of all that had happened in our family, our younger son was still studying to pass his test to become a Jehovah's Witness. The man who was studying with him condemned the crusade so harshly that I really believe our son came with me to spite him. We attended nearly every night and my husband went a few times. My friend who had been a Witness and her husband were also able to attend. Our younger son had never before heard the salvation message, been in a church, or even heard a hymn. He was impressed to know that Christ was indeed "The way, the truth and the life." He went forward and accepted Christ as his personal Savior and later got his uncle, Millard Bedwell, a minister in Idaho, to baptize him. The pastor assigned as his counsellor was the same one we had called on as Witnesses, Pastor Dell. This must also have been of God, for at that stage if I had gone to a church that had not been a Bible-believing, Bible-teaching church, I might never have tried again.

Pastor Dell had the greatest patience. He never pushed or ridiculed but was always there to help. I was starved for the Word of God and now I had help. He loaned me books, several at a time. I read them and asked to pass them on to my friend and her daughters. I still studied daily and prayed. One of the greatest helps I had was the Witnesses' Kingdom Interlinear Translation. It has the Greek on the left of the page and the Watchtower translation on the right. It really shows how the Witnesses have corrupted the Word of God to prove their erroneous doctrines. I compared translations and I asked our pastor and my brother-in-law to look up Greek words for me. I studied all the fundamental doctrines. I studied several books against the Witnesses. I couldn't seem to learn enough of the pure truth. It is difficult for one who has learned the whole Bible wrong to separate the good spiritual food from the tainted.

When I first went to church, I couldn't keep from crying when I heard the hymns. I had missed all this so much even though I had never gone to a church like this before. I felt like shaking the others and telling them to appreciate what they had and to use it. I am grateful for the painful lessons I learned, because now I really appreciate my blessings.

My husband and I both went forward and rededicated our lives to Christ and were baptized and joined our church. Our younger son is attending Appalachian Bible Institute. I pray daily for the others in our family and have the assurance that nothing is too big for God to handle, and that no deceived person is too small for Him to care about.

Our minister now is Pastor Cooper. He has really helped us mature. I couldn't begin to tell all the ways in which I know that the Lord has led. I have learned that I must surrender

56

my will to God and that prayers are answered. I still try to take over and do things myself at times, but I am slowly learning to really trust the Lord with everything in my life.

In the years since leaving the Watchtower Society I have been talked about and persecuted, and some family situations have hurt, but nothing really matters compared to the inner peace that the Holy Spirit brings. Christ is the only way to salvation, not a church, but I really understand the importance of gathering together in a Bible-believing church for spiritual strength and for encouragement.

I was so thankful for all that the Lord had done for me that I promised I would help others if I could, yet I may have had some reservations in this prayer. I thought the Lord would realize that I was limited, being a woman and a disorganized person. Though I am disfellowshiped and Jehovah's Witnesses shun me, still the Lord has used me, especially with those who are being drawn into studies with the Witnesses. I have bought and given away dozens of good books. I write my testimony and send tracts and booklets. When I think I have done all I can, there is always another way that opens up to witness and help many of my former deceived brothers and sisters and their new potential converts.

I would advise anyone leaving a cult to pray earnestly for the guidance and protection of the Holy Spirit, because I am always amazed to see how the devil fights for his own. One of his most common weapons seems to be to offer another of his cults to deceive them further. I know people personally who have been demonically attacked when they attempted to come free on their own. I'm thankful too, that as hard as it was and after the way I rejected and grieved the Holy Spirit in my ignorance, I have been spared further confusion by the cults or demonic interference.

As I know from experience, even a saved person can be

deceived into serving Satan. The only protection is to put on the full armor of God (Eph. 6). Read your Bible. Put faith in prayer. Surrender your whole life to the Lord.

Christian, prepare yourself, then talk kindly to the Jehovah's Witness at your door. Pray for his salvation and that his eyes may be opened.

**William and Joan Cetnar**

VII

## AN INSIDE VIEW OF THE WATCHTOWER SOCIETY

by

William and Joan Cetnar

The August 7, 1964, issue of the *Register* (Orange County, Calif.) carried an article headlined: "Dad Aids in Ban of Jehovah's Witness." The story by Bill Farr reported on the recent disfellowshiping of my wife, and my earlier similar experience, in December, 1962. My "heresy" was questioning the Witnesses' ban on blood transfusion; my wife's was "apostasy" —she had attended one of my talks on the Witnesses. My real break from the Jehovah's Witnesses, however, was not the result of being disfellowshiped, but rather the effect of arriving at the answer to what I considered the most important question of life: "Was the Watchtower Bible and Tract Society, the governing body of the Jehovah's Witnesses, God's organization?" My experiences and investigations while working at

59

the headquarters of this Society, and afterward in the local Kingdom Hall, convinced me that its claim to God's selection was baseless presumption. Further examination has strengthened this conviction.

My story, and that of my wife Joan, presents our search for truth, our dedication to what we believed to be true, our subsequent disillusionment, and our discovery, through God's leading, of peace—not in an organization—but in a personal relationship with Jesus Christ.

\* \* \* \* \*

By William Cetnar

I was born in Ambridge, Pennsylvania, a few months before the stock market crash of 1929. My parents were Catholic, and as a young man, Dad had even considered becoming a priest. About the time of my birth my mother became disillusioned with Catholicism because of the questionable behavior of the local priest. She seriously questioned whether the Catholic Church was *really* God's representative on earth. This disenchantment produced a vacuum which prepared the way for the visits of Jehovah's Witnesses and the acceptance of their teachings. My mother became convinced that Catholic doctrines were wrong, and she tried to get my dad to attend Witness meetings with her, but he refused. In fact, he said, "We're getting out of one mess and going into another!" But it wasn't long before my father also became interested in the Witnesses because one of his school friends was one.

My first recollections about the Watchtower Society are of the Washington, D. C., convention in 1935. Judge Rutherford was mentioned as the president of God's theocratic organization on earth.[1] I was led to understand that whatever came

---

1. I found out after leaving the Society that Rutherford's title of "judge" was based upon his acting as a stand-in for the regular judge

60

from the Society was not to be questioned, for it was God's channel for all Bible understanding.

In 1937, after two years of attending meetings three times a week and studying the book *The Harp of God*, I prayed a sincere and fervent prayer: "Father, whatever you want me to do, I dedicate my life to your service." At the convention in Columbus, Ohio, that year, when Judge Rutherford appeared, I broke away from my folks, ran under the usher's canes, and grabbed his coat. What a thrill! In my young mind his image was so glorified; he was the greatest fighter for Jehovah God and Jesus Christ that the world had ever seen. Whatever the Judge said was true.

It was in the same year that I witnessed the persecution of Jehovah's Witnesses. They were manhandled and some of their cars were overturned. I saw a sign ripped off my father's car. This treatment caused some Witnesses to leave the movement, but the ones who remained became more fervent and united in the work. Soon after this my parents were arrested and put in jail in Monessen, Pennsylvania, for carrying signs which declared: "Religion is a Snare and a Racket." Later I realized that my parents were not persecuted for "righteousness sake," as we believed at the time. If their signs had stated "False Religion is a Snare and a Racket," they would not have been persecuted. I still remember shoving bananas through the prison bars to my folks and others in the jail. My parents were released after several days.

In 1940 I was baptized at the Detroit convention. Baptism was an outward sign of my dedication to Jehovah. In 1943, as a junior high school student, I became a summer pioneer,

---

when he was ill, which amounted to about four days of service. He was never elected or appointed to a judgeship. See William J. Whalen, *Armageddon Around the Corner* (New York: The John Day Co., 1962), p. 49.

putting in 150 hours a month in the service. I did this for four years. Although I was only thirteen years of age, I was appointed advertising servant, which meant that I was in charge of the magazines, sound equipment, and phonographs. I set up the sound system for our park programs and played music before and after the meetings. I was given this responsibility because my dedication was recognized. I was very serious concerning my life as a Jehovah's Witness. When the Theocratic Ministry School was begun, I enrolled and I remember giving my first talk on the name "Jehovah." I did not know then that "Jehovah" was an "erroneous" or "false reading" (see *The American College Dictionary* and *Webster's New Collegiate Dictionary*, 1973 ed.).

In my house-to-house calling I was very rarely challenged on my beliefs. I felt so confident that what I had been taught was true that I actually welcomed opposition. Occasionally a person would ask me if I had been "born again." I replied "yes," and thought to myself, "Now let's talk about something important." The expression had little meaning to me.

By 1947 two questions had become a real concern. Was it wrong to serve in the armed services? Was the Watchtower Bible and Tract Society God's organization? The second question was the most important. I knew many non-Witness individuals whom I respected for their abilities, knowledge of the Bible, intelligence, and obvious love for God. I wondered why God chose only the Society as his organization and would destroy all other groups and individuals. What made the Watchtower leaders different? I wanted to see this for myself. I reasoned that if I went to Bethel and worked there I could actually sit down and talk with these leaders. The question of serving in the armed forces would also be taken care of, for I would have a 4-D classification. I had tried to get into Bethel as early as 1943 by sending letters to headquarters. I continued writing for several years. The replies from the president's office stated that I should wait—at least until I finished high school. One of the requirements at Bethel was that a person could not get married while serving there. It was nothing for me to promise this in expectation of serving in the headquarters of God's visible organization.

In 1947, at the age of 18, I went into full-time pioneer service. My first assignment was in Beverly Hills, California, where I met Jack Benny and other celebrities. I started some Bible studies with some well-known people. Then I was asked by the Society to go to Pacific Grove, California, to pioneer there. From there, in the spring of 1950, I was invited to go to work at Bethel.

My first assignment at Watchtower headquarters was as a waiter, and after six weeks I was transferred to the Circulation Department of the offices at 117 Adams Street. About six months later I was asked to work in the Service Department under T. J. Sullivan. "What a privilege," I thought. Among other things, this department organized congregations, approved circuit assemblies, and appointed servants. It also handled problems and answered Bible questions submitted by the congregations and acted as a court of appeals in disfellowshiping cases. My area of responsibility was one-third of the United States, from the Mason-Dixon Line south, and over to Texas. Often replies involved no more than sending out individually typed form letters or referring people to the appropriate Watchtower publications for Society policy. If a letter came to my desk which I could not answer, I consulted with T. J. Sullivan. Sometimes he would check with Vice-president Fred Franz or President Nathan Knorr. Franz usually answered matters of biblical policy and Knorr dealt with organizational matters.

### "Vaccination is a direct violation of the law of Jehovah God."

In December, 1951, when President Knorr came to review my department, I had about thirty letters on my desk from parents who had asked if it was against God's law to allow their children to have smallpox vaccinations as required by law for admittance into public schools. The Society's viewpoint on the matter had been clearly stated years before: ". . . As vaccination is a direct injection of animal matter in the blood stream vaccination is a direct violation of the law of Jehovah God" (*The Golden Age*, April 24, 1935, p. 465). My answer to these letters should have been a simple matter, but I did not have confidence in the Society's position on this point. After some questions concerning my work, Knorr asked, "What are those letters there on your desk?" I answered to the effect that I was having a problem answering them because I did not feel that the Society's policy on vaccination was correct. He replied, "It is not for you to determine policy." After our conversation I left for Pittsburgh, Pennsylvania, to give a talk. When I returned I found that the letters on my desk had been answered.

Later I visited the Lederle Laboratories, which made the smallpox vaccine, and found that my suspicions were correct. Although the Society taught that vaccinations violated God's law because they put animal blood into humans, I found that this was not true. The vaccine was made by a process known as avianization, in which the vaccine was cultured in the developing chick embryo and did not involve blood at all. On my return to headquarters I sent a memo to the president concerning my discovery, but it was never acknowledged.

### " 'God changed His mind' . . . April 15, 1952"

To my surprise, "God changed His mind" in a letter dated

64

April 15, 1952; in the letter the Society, speaking for God, reversed itself concerning vaccinations as "a direct violation of the law of Jehovah God." Among other things, this letter stated that "the matter of vaccination is one for the individual that has to face it to decide for himself. . . . Hence all objection to vaccination on Scriptural grounds seems to be lacking." When this change came about, I thought, as many other Witnesses did, that God's organization changed when it found something wrong. What I should have thought was: how could they have taught and paraded error as the "law of Jehovah" for so long? The erroneous ban on vaccinations had created some real problems. For example, before a child could attend first grade in the public schools he had to present a smallpox vaccination certificate. How could this be accomplished by the Witnesses who believed that vaccination was against God's law? My wife's parents did what many other Witness parents were doctrinally constrained to do. They took her to a doctor who simulated a vaccination on her leg by the use of acid. He signed the certificate and she had no trouble getting into school. Joan's cousin also had a similar "vaccination," but unfortunately the doctor accidentally spilled the acid on her leg. She carries the scar to this day. I was told that A. E. Ilett, the Bethel doctor, filled out certificates without vaccinations. This must have been the case, because without vaccinations Witness missionaries could not leave the country and they got certificates somewhere. In fact, I was told by one of the brothers that the Society was about to get into trouble on this matter and that is what produced the changed policy. I personally received a smallpox vaccination, but my brother and sister did not.

Another problem which developed was explained by a long-time Witness, A. H. Macmillan, in his book *Faith on the March*. A number of Witnesses had been denied draft exemptions as ministers and were placed in federal prisons. An order had been received from the Health Department that all men in these prisons had to be vaccinated. Witnesses in one prison who refused vaccination were placed in solitary confinement. Macmillan asked for and received permission to speak to these men. In the two-hour discussion which followed, it is interesting to read how Macmillan actually contradicted the arguments which had been employed in support of the Witnesses' position against vaccination (see p. 189). He also did not explain that the men were actually following Society policy in their stand. The men accepted the vaccinations.

What is the significance of this vaccination position held by the Society until 1952? Thousands of Witness parents and children were placed in the position of keeping "God's law" (the erroneous Watchtower dictum) and lying to school authorities. Men were needlessly in solitary confinement because of the error of the Society. Why did the official position of the Society not change until 1952? Will a discovery of erroneous teaching also be found in the Society's ban on blood transfusions? The problem on this point is that thousands will have already sacrificed their lives on the altar of Watchtower error.

### "See that Cadillac across the street—I gave that to Knorr and he can have another any time he wants one."

Another experience which caused me to question that the Watchtower Society was God's organization relates to Anton Koerber. I can still remember my father talking about him after the Washington, D. C., convention in 1935. Koerber was in charge of the sound equipment at the convention and for some reason had a falling out with Judge Rutherford. When Anton returned to Bethel, he found that he had been put out of the building and excommunicated from the Society. He went back into real estate and was very successful, amassing a

William Cetnar at the reception desk at 117 Adams Street, Brooklyn

T. J. Sullivan, Service Department director, who told William Cetnar to tell Anton Koerber he "could not be a pioneer"

fortune. Up until the year 1952, all I had heard of him was bad. He was a man who was an unfaithful servant, who went against God's theocratic organization, and who was disfellowshiped as a result.

In 1952 Anton Koerber contacted the Society and told those in authority that he wanted to become a full-time pioneer. His initial request was rejected because of his rebellion in the past. He next appeared at Bethel and I was told by T. J. Sullivan that I should go down to the eighth-floor lobby and make it clear to him that he could not be a pioneer. I went down to meet Mr. Koerber and found an elderly man who was not well. He asked me if he could be appointed a pioneer. I told him again that this was impossible because of his past history, and suggested, "You know, Anton, if you really love Jehovah you should serve Him for as many hours as you can without the title. You are merely being denied the title, not the privilege of service." He was not satisfied with this answer and indicated that he would pursue the matter further. As he shook my hand, he left a ten-dollar bill in it.

I reported back to T. J. Sullivan that Anton was not satisfied with my answer and stated that I wished that someone else would talk with him. So A. H. Macmillan was sent to convey the same message. I sat in on the session between Macmillan and Koerber. It was a thorough "chewing out"; Koerber was told that he was a selfish man who only wanted a title and that he would not get one. If he wanted to do something, he could be a congregational publisher. Macmillan was much more severe than I had been.

A day or two later when I went to the Bethel dining hall for dinner, I was dumbfounded, for there in the seat next to N. H. Knorr, as his guest, was Anton Koerber. I left the room after the meal almost not believing what I had seen. I went into the lobby and Koerber called me over and pointed out the window

William Cetnar (right) and George D. Gangas, one member of the New World Bible Translation Committee

Three Service Department desks: William Cetnar (left rear), Service South; Joe Tomlanovich (left front), Service East; and Fred Rusk, Service West

to a new car parked at the curb, and said: "See that Cadillac across the street—I gave that to Knorr and he can have another any time he wants one." Some years later when I spoke of this experience to G. Russell Pollock, he related how Koerber had approached the Dawn Bible Students in 1951 shortly before his contact with the Watchtower Society. The information was presented in a letter from Pollock dated November 15, 1971:

> . . . Anton Koerber sent *The Dawn* a check for $2,000 and asked to have a conference with the trustees of the Dawn. We had the meeting with him at our General Convention in 1951. He offered money to the Dawn if they would establish an organization similar in structure to that of Jehovah's Witnesses. That is, being controlled from a central headquarters. This discussion continued at various times by telephone from his home in Florida. We, of course, could not accept his terms of cooperation. As Bill stated: "the 'evil servant' refused his bribe but the 'faithful and wise' accepted it." The foregoing is true and can be verified. [See the entire letter, Figure 3.]

But the conclusion of this account is even more significant. Anton Koerber, who had been turned down as a pioneer, a relatively insignificant position, was made a *circuit servant*, a position normally selected from the ranks of faithful pioneers! In 1953 he was made a chairman of the international convention at Yankee Stadium. He died on November 19, 1967, and the May 15, 1968, *Watchtower* carried "The life story of ANTON KOERBER as told by his friends" (pp. 313-318). (The article quickly moves over the period between 1935 and 1952 in a sentence which does not give any hint of what really took place.)

*The Watchtower's* story on him does emphasize that he "was extremely generous in a material way . . ." (p. 318). In his discourse at Dodger Stadium (July 22, 1973), Vice-

Figure 3

Gordon Russell Pollock
627 N. Foothill Road
Beverly Hills, Calif.,90210
November 15, 1971

Mr. & Mrs. Carl R. Howell
Route One
Saylorsburg, Pennsylvania

Dear Brother & Sister Howell:

Some forty years have passed since we have seen each other out
there on the farm near Kunkletown. This letter is really at the request
of your daughter, Joan, and son-in-law, Bill. In a recent conversation
Anton Koerber was mentioned. Bill related what had happened in 1951
when he was in the service department at Bethel. Anton Koerber requested
the Society to appoint him as apioneer. Bill was told by Bro. Sullivan
that Anton Koerber could not be appointed as a pioneer due to his course
of action toward the Society in 1935. Bill related this information to
Anton Koerber and suggested that he serve the Lord with as many hours as
possible but without the title "pioneer".

Anton then pursued the matter by getting in touch with N. H. Knorr.
Anton presented Knorr with a new cadillac and was soon appointed a circuit
servant. Anton meeting Bill in the Bethel lobby said: "See that cadillac
across the street — I gave that to Knorr and he can have another anytime
he wants one." The following year he was chairman at Yankee Stadium convention.

Then, I told Bill: "Let me fill you in on that story." In the same
year Anton Koerber sent The Dawn a check for $2,000 and asked to have a
conference with the trustees of the Dawn. We had the meeting with him at
our General Convention in 1951. He offered money to the Dawn if they would
establish an organization similar in structure to that of Jehovah's Witnesses.
That is, being controlled from a central headquarters. This discussion continued at various times by telephone from his home in Florida. We of course,
could not accept his terms of cooperation. As Bill stated: "the 'evil
servant' refused a bribe but the 'faithful and wise' accepted it." The
foregoing is true and can be verified.

Hope this letter finds you in good health and feel free to write to
me at any time, as I would be happy to hear from you.

Sincerely, *By His Grace,*

*Brother G R Pollock*

Gordon Russell Pollock

71

president Franz actually used Anton Koerber as an example of a man "who saw the need of concentrating upon the spiritual values and following faithfully in the steps of the Lord Jesus Christ." He was commended for turning down a business opportunity which in under a year could have made him a million dollars. "Why? Because he did not want to interrupt his contribution of full time in the ministry of Jehovah God."

The facts indicate that Anton Koerber would have been just as happy with the Dawn Bible Students ("evil servant") as with the Watchtower Society ("faithful and wise"), as long as he could receive public plaudits.

### "I had no background for an objective evaluation of the evidence. The guiding principle was conformity to the Society's position."

In addition to my work in the Service Department, discussed previously, I was also assigned to do research for articles and worked under Bill Wheeler of the Editorial Department in this capacity. What were my qualifications for such work? None. Often all I knew about a subject was what I was able to gain by reading various treatments on it. I had no background for an objective evaluation of the evidence. The guiding principle was conformity to the Society's position. If material agreed, it was utilized; if it did not, it was rejected. From my observations at headquarters, I would conclude that this lack of qualifications would characterize the majority of the editorial staff. Most had no training beyond high school. This is also true of the Society's president, N. H. Knorr, who entered Bethel service upon graduation from high school and worked his way up through the ranks. Witnesses are discouraged from going to college and from reading non-Witness books, for, we were told, "These were put together by worldly men." Recently, a talk was given at a convention held at the Forum in

72

Inglewood, California, where Witnesses were told by A. D. Schroeder that they should not read non-Witness publications because this would take hours of time which could be better spent in Witness materials or service. They were told that if the books contained anything worthwhile, the Society would take it out, condense it, and give them something they could read in a few minutes. This actually was a subtle form of censorship, since it was already true that any books about the Society by former Witnesses could not be read. Witnesses were being restricted to reading nothing but Watchtower materials.

In addition to research projects I worked on Theocratic Ministry School talk outlines, and during 1951 and 1952 I wrote a monthly article for the *Informant* (now *Kingdom Ministry*). Because I was on the Bethel speaker's staff, I spoke at a number of Kingdom Halls and at several of the large conventions. For approximately a year I wrote and produced a half-hour program for the Society-owned radio station WBBR.

### "If I were on the translation committee, I would want my name to be kept secret also."

Work on the New World Translation was being done and much was completed while I was in Bethel. The translation committee requested that the names of the translators remain secret even after their deaths (*Jehovah's Witnesses in the Divine Purpose*, p. 258). Knowing who the translators were, for this was common knowledge at Bethel, if I were on the translation committee, I would want my name to be kept secret also. The reason for the anonymity of the translators was twofold: (1) the qualifications of the translators could not be checked and evaluated, and (2) there would be no one to assume the responsibility for the translation. However, when Franz was asked in a courtroom in Scotland, "Why the secrecy?" he said,

"Because the committee of translation wanted it to remain anonymous and not seek any glory or honour at the making of a translation, and having any names attached thereto." The attorney replied, "Writers of books and translators do not always get glory and honour for their efforts, do they?" (*Pursuer's Proof of Douglas Walsh vs. The Right Honourable James Latham, M.P., P.C.*, Scottish Court of Sessions, November, 1954, p. 92).

Would it not be of the utmost importance to know the men, their qualifications and credentials—men to whom we would entrust our spiritual lives? We certainly would not put trust in a surgeon who would not give us his name or credentials. It was interesting to me that at Bethel these translators took no precautions to keep themselves anonymous. They would get up from the dining room table early and all leave together in the president's limousine for Staten Island. There they would remain, sometimes absent from Bethel for weeks at a time.[2]

From my observation, N. H. Knorr, F. W. Franz, A. D. Schroeder, G. D. Gangas, and M. Henschel met together in these translation sessions. Aside from Vice-president Franz (and his training was limited), none of the committee members had adequate schooling or background to function as critical Bible translators. Franz's ability to do a scholarly job of translating Hebrew is open to serious question. This came out in the Scottish Court of Sessions in November, 1954. The following exchange of questions and answers between the attorney and Franz is taken from the trial transcript:

Q. Have you also made yourself familiar with Hebrew?

---

2. This crafty procedure is not new with the Society. In fact, the Watchtower Society attributes all the "new light" to an anonymous body called the "remnant" (an abstract scapegoat). Yet no one has a list of the names of the "faithful and wise" or "remnant." No one knows who the "remnant" really is. Nor has the "remnant" met in convention to decide on any Society policy or "new light."

74

A. Yes. . . .
Q. So that you have a substantial linguistic apparatus at your command?
A. Yes, for use in my biblical work.
Q. I think you are able to read and follow the Bible in Hebrew, Greek, Latin, Spanish, Portuguese, German and French?
A. Yes [*Pursuer's Proof*, p. 7]. . . .
Q. You, yourself, read and speak Hebrew, do you?
A. I do not speak Hebrew.
Q. You do not?
A. No.
Q. Can you, yourself, translate that into Hebrew?
A. Which?
Q. That fourth verse of second chapter of Genesis?
A. You mean here?
Q. Yes?
A. No. I wouldn't attempt to do that [*Pursuer's Proof*, p. 61].

What Franz "wouldn't attempt" to translate into Hebrew was a simple exercise with which an average first- or second-year Hebrew student in seminary would have no difficulty. This conclusion was stated by a qualified teacher of Hebrew.

Because of the inadequacy of the translators, the translations which resulted were, in many cases, not those which were accurate renderings of the original languages, but rather they conveyed what the Witnesses believed. This is verified by many qualified Bible scholars, among them Dr. Anthony Hoekema, who commented:

> . . . Their *New World Translation* of the Bible is by no means an objective rendering of the sacred text into Modern English, but is *a biased translation in which many of the peculiar teachings of the Watchtower Society are smuggled into the text of the Bible itself* [*The Four Major Cults*, pp. 238, 239].

In March, 1954, I was assigned to interview the well-known Bible translator, Dr. Edgar J. Goodspeed, for his evaluation of the first volume of the *New World Translation of the Hebrew Scriptures.* I was to try to get his endorsement of it. During the two-hour visit with him it was obvious that he knew the volume well, because he could cite the page numbers where the readings he objected to were found. One reading he pointed out as especially awkward and grammatically poor was in Judges 14:3 (p. 803, first edition), where Samson is made to say: "Her get for me. . . ." As I left, Dr. Goodspeed was asked if he could recommend the translation for the general public. He answered, "No, I'm afraid I could not do that. The grammar is regrettable. Be careful on the grammar. Be sure you have that right."

### "When it gets off the sixth floor IT IS THE TRUTH."

When I had gone to Bethel in 1950, the Society's position against the transfusion of blood had not as yet become a major issue. The doctrine would receive more attention and newspaper coverage after this time. Several cases of Witnesses who refused transfusions came to my attention while at Bethel. I checked into the scriptural support which we used and concluded that our position was wrong. I argued the matter with Colin Quackenbush, who was then the editor of *Awake!* Other members of the Editorial Department also knew how I felt personally. I may have lost prestige in their eyes, but I was not disfellowshiped, which certainly would have been the case had I taken the same position in a local Kingdom Hall. I accepted what the Bible said in Acts 15 on the matter of not drinking blood. But I also knew that it was not against God's law because of what Jesus said in Mark 7:15: " 'There is nothing from outside a man that passes into him that can defile him; but the things that issue forth out of a man are the things that defile a man' " (NWT).

76

Probably because of my disagreement with the Society's policy on blood transfusion I was reassigned from my job in the Service Department and made a receptionist at 117 Adams Street. This was a branch of the Service Department's activities and here I still had a responsible position as I screened the people who came into the lobby of the building. It was while working as receptionist that I first met Mr. Walter R. Martin, author of *The Kingdom of the Cults,* an excellent aid to anyone involved with the cults. Unknown to Mr. Martin, in spite of our confrontation he had planted seeds of truth that helped me in the understanding of Christian theology. He asked me to read Isaiah 44:6 where Jehovah declares that He alone is the First and Last and the *only* God, which eliminates forever any confusion as to there being *two* Firsts and Lasts. Since Jehovah is the only God, then how can the *logos* be "a god," a lesser god than Jehovah, as Jehovah's Witnesses declare?

Revelation 1:17, 18 and 2:8 add further weight to the deity of Christ, for they reveal Him as the First and the Last, who died and lives forever. In Revelation 22:13 Jesus said: "I am Alpha and Omega, the beginning and the end, the first and the last." I had to accept this or deny the authority of the Scriptures. We met twenty years later and he was happy to hear of my coming out of the Society.

At headquarters the men of the Editorial Department often had differences of opinion. Each had to carefully "pad" his differences so as not to lose a position or be considered a heretic. President Knorr made a very significant and revealing statement in 1952 after some of the brothers in editorial had argued over a doctrinal matter. He stated, "Brothers, you can argue all you want about it, but when it gets off the sixth floor *it is the truth.*" What he was saying was that once it was in print (the presses were on the sixth floor), it is the truth and we had to stand unitedly behind it. Franz in court admitted

77

the same; however, he did not speak the truth when he said there were no differences of opinion.

> Q. But am I right that the Board of Directors do at some stage consider it ["it" meaning any proposed statement for publication].
> A. They all consider it.
> Q. And vote upon it if need be?
> A. They express their opinions upon it.
> Q. And vote upon it if need be?
> A. There is no voting upon it. If it is published it is accepted.
> Q. But before it is published how is it decided upon if there be a difference of view in the Board of Directors.
> A. There is no difference of view in the Board of Directors.
> Q. Never?
> A. After the matter is published there is agreement [*Pursuers Proof*, p. 106].

**"The Jonadabs could not be killed. . . . The brothers were completely surprised that Jehovah would not protect the Jonadabs."**

Often I have been asked, "What gives the Witnesses such fervent zeal to propagate their beliefs and even to die for them?" The answer is that Jehovah's Witnesses believe that the Society has the authority to speak for God and that they are serving and dying for God. What the Society teaches is clearly reflected in the Witnesses' attitude. An interesting conversation took place in 1955, when Conrad Franke, who was Branch Servant of Germany, and F. C. S. Hoffmann, who was Branch Servant of Switzerland, got together with a few other brothers in my Bethel room. In the course of the conversation I asked Brother Franke about a matter which related to the special protection of the Jehovah's Witnesses in concentration camps during the Second World War. I had been told that during the late thirties, Judge Rutherford spoke at a convention in Germany and told the brethren there that in times of danger they could expect special protection from God if they were Jonadabs.

Belief in God's protection helps to explain how two thousand Jehovah's Witnesses fearlessly stood and died before Hitler's firing squads. They had been told that God would stop the bullets. It had been explained that the Jonadabs could not be killed because of their expectation of going through Armageddon, but the remnant (144,000) should expect persecution that would end in death. Brother Franke explained that before this announcement about *eighty percent* of the German brethren felt that they were of the remnant. After Rutherford's talk and the publication of the article, "His Name," in *The Watchtower,* the number of those claiming to be members of the remnant dropped to just *twenty percent!*

The illusion of protection was completely shattered by an experience during the war. Brother Franke related how five German brothers, who were of the "protected Jonadabs," refused to take shelter during an air raid by the RAF. One of the bombs made a direct hit just as they were studying the daily text, and they were killed instantly. Understandably, this incident changed the beliefs of the Jehovah's Witnesses in Germany. The brethren who heard of this were completely surprised that God would not protect the Jonadabs as Judge Rutherford had declared. To make sure that I had understood the story accurately, I corresponded with Conrad Franke and his verification came in a letter to me dated, August 27, 1963.

### "Charles De Wilda died on a park bench after four decades of faithful service."

One of the tragic episodes which unfolded during my service at Watchtower headquarters concerned Charles De Wilda. Charlie, as we all called him, had deserted from the Cavalry after World War I and in looking for a job he had walked into headquarters and asked for work. He was told that he could have a job, but that the pay was only room and board and $20.00 a month. He took the offer and had worked for over thirty years by the time I met him. By now Charlie was an old man and a little senile, but still a very hard worker. President Knorr often used him as an example of how much work could be accomplished. He had been the best bookbinder on the fourth floor.

Charlie, like all other Bethel workers, was not allowed to get married *if he wished to remain in Bethel.* Knorr had often stressed this policy and Charlie resented it. But in 1952, in violation of the rule, President Knorr married Audrey Mock, one of the sisters at Bethel. Several years after the marriage Charlie went to President Knorr and told him that he had broken his own rule and that he ought to resign. He also said to him, "You preach more about love than anyone in the world I know, but practice it least!" As punishment for this confrontation, Charlie was removed from his assigned seat in the dining hall and placed in a remote corner. The excuse for this was that he had used foul language. It was obvious that he was being punished. He refused to stay in this new seat and returned to his usual table. It was made so difficult for him at Bethel that he packed his few belongings and walked out into the outside world. Bethel had been his entire life. He even spent his vacations there. He didn't know where he was going, and he had no place to go, but to him anything was better than Bethel at the time. I met him later; he was staying in a horrible flophouse at fifty cents a night. After he ran out of funds, he began to ask Bethel workers and other Witnesses for money to buy meals. I gave him some to meet his need. Bethel workers were told not to give Charlie any money, and a letter saying the same thing was sent out from headquarters to congregations in the area. This was an effort to force him to return. The last I heard was that Charles

De Wilda died on a park bench. This is the reward a man gets after four decades of faithful service in "God's organization" because he pointed out an obvious inconsistency. This was one example that revealed to me how little love there really was at headquarters for the people working there.

Another incident comes to mind. One young man had four of his fingers cut off in the paper trimmer. Because he was no more use in the factory, he was sent out as a pioneer to fend for himself. His accident was not compensated because the insurance to cover such accidents was "too expensive." I could not accept such an explanation for not having insurance. Why? I was told by Myron Quackenbush (Society controller) that the total cost of manufacturing a book like *Let God Be True* (over 300 pages), which sold for fifty cents, was only seven cents! We were printing each day a stack of these books as high as the Empire State Building! There were similar profits in the publishing of other materials. In addition, thousands of Jehovah's Witnesses die each year and will their estates to the Watchtower Society. Many thousands more donate money on a regular basis each year. There are many who give large sums as special gifts. I had such a gift given to me for the Society one day by a sailor who disembarked from his ship, made his way to Brooklyn, left a thousand dollars with me, and asked that the gift remain anonymous. There is also great profit in the conventions held each year, through offerings and through the food concessions. For example, at Yankee Stadium in 1958, there were over 250,000 people at the convention. The prices on the food were moderate, but the labor was free, and what food was not donated by Witnesses, was bought at wholesale prices. I once figured that a person could become wealthy on the sale of pies alone. I concluded this on the basis of knowing what the pies cost and what they were sold for in slices.

The excuse of insurance being "too expensive" to cover the factory workers in case of accident did not hold up to investigation, and was just another indication of the lack of concern for the welfare of the headquarters workers.

**"We couldn't afford to care for the Witness girl properly. . . . This callous decision had cost her her life."**

Another incident shook my faith in the organization and its leadership. In 1956 or 1957 two young ladies came from Thailand to receive missionary training at Gilead. The pressures of learning the language and the other necessary subjects caused one of them to suffer a mental breakdown. She was periodically driven by an overpowering compulsion which caused her to take off her clothes and run through the building. She was sent to Bethel with the hope that she might be able to relax some and recuperate. But her condition grew worse and she tried to commit suicide by attempting to jump from the Bethel home.

President Knorr told Worth Thornton, transportation secretary, to send the girl back to Thailand the cheapest way, as soon as possible. Arrangements were made to place her on a train to San Fransisco and there she would board a ship for Thailand. When she learned of this she begged to be placed on a plane, or to have another missionary accompany her. She explained that when she had the spells, she could not control herself and if she were on a ship, she might jump overboard. Both of her requests were refused as being too expensive. Worth Thornton was very upset about this, a fact known to me because I had discussions with him about the matter.

The girl was put on the train, and at San Francisco she boarded a merchant vessel. When the ship passed Hawaii, she had one of her seizures and jumped overboard. The ship circled back to search for her, but she was never found. Possibly she had been eaten by sharks. The ship notified the Society by radiogram about what had happened, and the message was received by Arthur Barnett, who was operating the switchboard at Bethel. Russell Kurzen, Bethel receptionist, also learned of the tragedy. Both men were shocked and they relayed the news to others in the Bethel family. President Knorr became very upset that the information had been given out, and both Arthur and Russell were removed from their positions.

This episode bothered me very much. There were sufficient funds available to provide first-class travel accommodations and every luxury for the president of the Society—but we couldn't afford to care for the Witness girl properly so that she could get home safely. This callous decision had cost her her life.

**"I resigned from Bethel in the summer of 1958. . . . I wanted to think things over."**

I had seen and experienced many things in my eight and one-half years in Watchtower headquarters. I resigned from Bethel in the summer of 1958, and at that time I had no desire to take any positions in the Society. Joan had completed her agreed term of service in Bethel and she also resigned. I was asked if I wanted to be a district or circuit servant, but I refused both of these. I didn't even want to be a pioneer. I wanted to think things over away from the pressures at headquarters.

I had a number of doubts concerning the Society as a result of my experiences at Bethel, but these did not cause me to turn away from the organization doctrinally; rather it was getting back into the Bible and checking out our teachings, and finding them contradictory to the Scriptures, which brought this about.

Joan and I were married in September, 1958. Our good

83

friend, Colin Quackenbush, former editor of *Awake!*, preached the sermon at our wedding. My father-in-law, Carl Howell, asked me what I wanted to do for a living. I answered, "All I have been trained to do is to preach." He said that I could work on his farm and Joan and I could have half of the house to live in. I accepted this offer and went to work on the farm, which was one of the finest in Pennsylvania. Carl and I got along beautifully and I enjoyed the work.

Gradually I got back into the Witness work, and I finally agreed to be Ministry School servant and then Bible study servant in the local congregation.

### "I was disfellowshiped for making my position on blood transfusion known."

My physical break from the Jehovah's Witnesses was precipitated when the grandparents of a young child who needed a blood transfusion, asked me what I would do if my child required one. I answered that I would let the doctor decide. Because of this answer the Headquarters' judicial committee called for me to report for a hearing at the Brodheadsville Kingdom Hall on the matter. The reason for my eventual disfellowshiping was the matter of blood transfusion; this is of special significance and should be explained in some detail.

The July 1, 1945, issue of *The Watchtower* presented the ban on blood transfusions. The paragraph from the article is quoted in full:

> Seeing, then, that the Most High and Holy God gave plain instructions as to the disposition of blood, in harmony with his everlasting covenant with Noah and all his descendants; and seeing that the use of blood that he authorized in order to furnish life to humankind was the use of it as a propitiation or atonement for sin; and seeing that it was to be done upon his holy altar or at his mercy seat, and not

by taking such blood directly into the human body; therefore it behooves all worshipers of Jehovah who seek eternal life in this new world of righteousness to respect the sanctity of blood and to conform themselves to God's righteous rulings concerning this vital matter [p. 201].

The transfusion ban was clear to my father-in-law and his cousin Hayden, for they had explained the Society's policy to a sister in the congregation, Mae Altemose, who said that if she needed a transfusion, she would receive it. She was called on the carpet and told that if she took a transfusion she could be disfellowshiped. What was really hypocritical was that in 1949, Joan's grandfather, William Kimmel, a member of the 144,000, *received* a blood transfusion, and her father, Carl Howell, the presiding minister and her uncle, Hayden Howell, both *gave* blood and also encouraged neighbors to do the same! They did this even though they knew the grandfather had leukemia!

When Joan's father was later confronted with this violation of "God's righteous rulings," he stated that the doctrine was "not very clear at the time." I replied, "It wasn't very clear when the president of Jehovah's Witnesses and other leaders came to your farm and ate at your table? And if it was not clear, couldn't you have phoned Brooklyn as you do on other questions?" Then I said to Carl, "I never gave a transfusion and I never received one. I was disfellowshiped for making my position on blood transfusion known." Those involved in the transfusion received by Joan's grandfather were not even scolded, although the matter was known.

### "Being disfellowshiped was probably the second most important day of my life."

Now, as I look back over my experience, I feel that being disfellowshiped was probably the second most important day of my life. The most important day was when I dedicated my

85

life to God. Why was being disfellowshiped of such consequence? Because it brought about a break from an organization
and system which I could no longer accept. It kept me from
wavering back and forth between what I knew to be true and
what I was expected to believe as a Witness. It also freed me
from the pressure of trying to keep dear Witness friends whom I
liked, by outwardly accepting untrue doctrines which I did not
like. Without the break of being disfellowshiped, I would have
been living a hypocritical life, the frustrating experience of many
Witnesses today.

The statement that many Witnesses are living hypocritical
lives is not just my opinion, but that which was clearly proven
by my own experiences and observations of the Witnesses I
knew. For example, at least six Witness friends came to me
after my disfellowshiping and said something like this: "Bill,
just say that you agree with them on blood transfusion; I
don't believe everything that is being taught either." A servant
in the congregation said, "Believe anything you want Bill,
but just stay with us." Over the years a number of Witnesses
had expressed other mental reservations they had regarding
Society teachings. On numerous occasions, too detailed and
lengthy to relate here, it was obvious to me that Witnesses
often were not concerned with what Jehovah God would think
of an action, but took care to keep from the attention of other
Witnesses any ideas they might have which were contrary to
Society policy. Obviously Society approval meant more than
the approval of God.

Another experience, which is typical of others, reinforces
the points made above. A servant in the Kingdom Hall where
I was a member told me of a study which he had been conducting with a certain family for about two years. I had
occasion to visit that same family and I inquired about the
brother. They indicated that they had not seen him for many

months and that he was not conducting a study there. This brother "conducted" his Bible study by simply filling out the time slip. He went into field service on Sundays by going to a local cafe and eating breakfast and reading his newspaper. It was my observation that many time slips were either false or padded. It was and is an easy matter to fill in a slip without putting in the time, especially when service is demanded.

### "If we were to leave, where else could we go?"

I am convinced that many Jehovah's Witnesses, who know much in the Society is wrong, are afraid to leave. They are ensnared by the question which the Society often presents to them: "If we were to leave it, where else could we go?" (*The Watchtower,* July 1, 1973, p. 404). Some who leave the organization, who are more Bible oriented, soon find Christ as their Savior. At least one who left Bethel, later worked with the Billy Graham organization, and others have become leaders in evangelical churches. These are the most reprehensible to the Society's leadership. They would rather have them leave the movement as skeptics or atheists.

I am personally very disappointed with the former leaders of Jehovah's Witnesses who no longer accept some of the doctrines of the Society; instead of taking a stand in opposition to that which is wrong, they take a neutral position, because of their fear of being disfellowshiped.[3] The Bible speaks to this point: "Therefore, to one who knows the right thing to do, and does not do it, to him it is sin" (James 4:17, New American Standard). As prominent Society representatives these men

---

3. For many former Jehovah's Witnesses, being disfellowshiped can be a traumatic experience. If the reader is in that position, or should it come at a later time, he should realize that he is not really disfellowshiped, for he can have fellowship with whomever he chooses. It is the Witnesses who cannot have fellowship with the ex-Witness— they are the ones who really have been disfellowshiped!

have given speeches and written articles. They have led others to refuse blood transfusions and to accept the claim that there was "Only One Right Religion"—the Jehovah's Witnesses. They have since changed their course, but they will not make their views public. They seem paralyzed into inaction, fearing what the Society might do, rather than fearing their ultimate accounting before Jehovah God.

Where can one go when he leaves the organization? Actually the answer is given in the very passage of Scripture the Witnesses often cite in posing the question, John 6:66-68:

> Owing to this many of his disciples went off to the things behind and would no longer walk with him. Therefore Jesus said to the twelve: "YOU do not want to go also, do YOU?" Simon Peter answered him: "Lord, whom shall we go away to? You have sayings of everlasting life" [NWT].

Where can one go? What can one do? The sincere seeker can go directly to the Lord Jesus Christ and ask Him for direction. He can read the Bible as it is written, without organizational understanding, asking the Holy Spirit of God to guide him "into all the truth" (John 16:13, NWT), just as Jesus said He would.

When was I "born again?" (John 3:3, 5, 7). I believe that this occurred in 1937, when I gave myself to God through Jesus Christ. At that time I wasn't praying to God to become a Jehovah's Witness. I acknowledged myself as a sinner and I realized that I needed Jesus Christ as my Savior. I wanted to do anything that God wanted me to do. At that time I didn't comprehend the sufficient provision that Christ had made for me in His death on Calvary, a provision that I could fully appropriate through simple faith.

Where do I stand now? I believe that I am saved through faith in the death of Christ for me. Salvation is a gift of God (Eph. 2:8, 9), not based upon what I can do, but rather upon

88

what Christ has already done. Salvation is not in an organization, but in a Person. Based on what the Bible clearly states, I
*know* that I have everlasting life (I John 5:13). A Jehovah's
Witness cannot say these things because he cannot see salvation outside of the organization.

God has blessed our family since we literally left all to
follow Him: religion, friends, parents, inheritance, home, job.
God has met all our needs as we took a stand for what was
right. He has also used our efforts to free other Witnesses from
the organization.

Often I have asked myself why I was allowed by God to
become involved with the Witnesses and to stay ensnared in
Watchtower error for so many years. Several ministers and
others have suggested, and I concur, that my experiences in
the Watchtower Society were for the benefit of others who
could be helped and delivered because of my contact. I pray
and direct every effort to this end. May Jehovah God and the
Lord Jesus Christ be glorified in this ministry.

\* \* \* \* \*

Since I left the Society in 1962, many former Jehovah's
Witnesses have urged me to publish these life incidents and the
experiences which occurred at Watchtower headquarters. My
initial reticence stemmed mainly from the view that all humans
are imperfect and therefore have committed imperfect acts.
However, it should be pointed out that the Watchtower leaders
have assumed the authority of speaking as the representatives
of Almighty God, and the obvious presumption and falsity of
this claim removed all reservations I had.

A key reason for my speaking out at this time is that the
issue is one of life and death. Jehovah's Witnesses and their
children, faced with the need of blood, should not be allowed
to die because of the ill-founded Watchtower precepts on blood
transfusion. It is partly a matter of my keeping a good con-

science; by keeping silent, I would in essence be giving assistance to a belief that risks the lives of needy people. I do not want the deaths of innocent children on my conscience.

After having read my account, many will conveniently dismiss much of what I say as being untrue. If this is the conclusion of the reader, I invite him to investigate these things for himself. There are many former Jehovah's Witnesses who can be of help, and on subjects not treated in my story there are many good books available for further study (see the Bibliography).

\* \* \* \* \*

## By Joan Cetnar

The Jehovah's Witnesses were certainly not strangers to our family. My great-grandparents, Sebastian and Catherine Kresge, the parents of S. S. Kresge[4] (of department store fame), became Bible Students (as they were known at that time) in the 1890's, through reading Pastor Russell's books. Two of her daughters married two of the Howell brothers; one was my grandfather. Both of my parents were, and still are, staunch Jehovah's Witnesses. Only young children in 1914, they lived through the prophetic failures of 1914, 1918, and 1925. My mother was active in distributing the book *Millions Now Living Will Never Die!* (published in 1920), which predicted the resurrection of Abraham, Isaac, and the other Old Testament patriarchs in 1925 and the establishment of the earthly phase of the kingdom. How definite were the predictions for that year? Let the reader judge from a quotation from this book:

---

4. S. S. Kresge and his family never became Jehovah's Witnesses, and family members with whom I am acquainted are active Christians.

90

. . . That period of time . . . would end in the fall of the year 1925, at which time the type ends and the great antitype must begin. What, then, should be expected to take place? In the type there must be a full restoration; therefore the great antitype must mark the beginning of restoration of all things. The chief thing to be restored is the human race to life; and since other Scriptures definitely fix the fact that there will be a restoration of Abraham, Isaac, Jacob and other faithful ones of old, and that these will have the first favor, we may expect 1925 to witness the return of these faithful men of Israel from the condition of death, being resurrected and fully restored to perfect humanity and made the visible, legal representatives of the new order of things on earth.

Messiah's kingdom once established, Jesus and his glorified church constituting the great Messiah, shall minister the blessings to the people they have so long desired and hoped for and prayed might come. . . .

As we have heretofore stated, the great jubilee cycle is due to begin in 1925. At that time the earthly phase of the kingdom shall be recognized . . . [pp. 88, 89; see figure 4].

I did not know of this predictive failure and others that the Society had made until *after* I had left the Witnesses. I asked my mother about the *Millions Now Living Will Never Die* campaign and if she had presented the 1925 speculation in her witnessing work. She said that she had, and then added, "But I didn't believe it!" This answer surprised me and I replied, "You don't believe it *now*, but you must have believed it then!"

I remember that when I went from door to door people told me that we had predicted the end of this world before. I would answer, "No, we didn't!" I concluded this was true because it is what my parents had told me in answer to questions on the subject.

My father was the congregational servant after the Kingdom

**Figure 4**

seventy jubilees kept. (Jeremiah 25:11; 2 Chronicles 36:17-21) A simple calculation of these jubilees brings us to this important fact: Seventy jubilees of fifty years each would be a total of 3500 years. That period of time beginning 1575 before A. D. 1 of necessity would end in the fall of the year 1925, at which time the type ends and the great antitype must begin. What, then, should we expect to take place? In the type there must be a full restoration; therefore the great antitype must mark the beginning of restoration of all things. The chief thing to be restored is the human race to life; and since other Scriptures definitely fix the fact that there will be a resurrection of Abraham, Isaac, Jacob and other faithful ones of old, and that these will have the first favor, we may expect 1925 to witness the return of these faithful men of Israel from the condition of death, being resurrected and fully restored to perfect humanity and made the visible, legal representatives of the new order of things on earth.

Messiah's kingdom once established, Jesus and his glorified church constituting the great Messiah, shall minister the blessings to the people they have so long desired and hoped for and prayed might come. And when that time comes, there will be peace and not war, as the prophet beautifully states: "In the last days it shall come to pass, that the mountain of the house of the Lord shall be established in the top of the mountains, and it shall be exalted above

the hills; and people shall flow unto it. And many nations shall come, and say, Come, and let us go up to the mountain of the Lord, and to the house of the God of Jacob; and he will teach us of his ways, and we will walk in his paths: for the law shall go forth of Zion, and the word *of the Lord from Jerusalem. And he shall judge* among many people, and rebuke strong nations afar off; and they shall beat their swords into plowshares, and their spears into pruninghooks; nation shall not life up a sword against nation, neither shall they learn war any more. But they shall sit every man under his vine and under his fig tree; and none shall make them afraid; for the mouth of the Lord of hosts hath spoken it." —Micah 4:1-4.

EARTHLY RULERS

As we have heretofore stated, the great jubilee cycle is due to begin in 1925. At that time the earthly phase of the kingdom shall be recognized. The Apostle Paul in the eleventh chapter of Hebrews names a long list of faithful men who died before the crucifixion of the Lord and before the beginning of the selection of the church. These can never be a part of the heavenly class; they had no heavenly hopes; but God has in store something good for them. They are to be resurrected as perfect men and constitute the princes or rulers in the earth, according to his promise. (Psalm 45:16; Isaiah 32:1; Matthew 8:11) Therefore we may confidently expect that 1925 will mark the return of Abraham,

Pages 88 and 89 of J. F. Rutherford's *Millions Now Living Will Never Die*, published in 1920. The predictions for 1925 were a failure.

Hall in Brodheadsville, Pennsylvania, was established in the early 1930's. I grew up going to meetings, assemblies, and conventions. I went to the Bible studies conducted in homes by my parents, and as soon as I could I read the Scriptures and helped my father conduct the studies. During the year, rain or shine, I spent time witnessing on street corners and in the house-to-house work. I mention these activities to indicate that I did not take my faith as a passive thing.

As I grew up, visitors from Watchtower headquarters were often at our home. Many Bethelites spent their vacations on our farm. Nathan Knorr and my parents have been friends for years, and I knew him as a friend of the family as well as the president of the Society.

During the time when flag saluting was compulsory, the principal of Chestnuthill Consolidated School was understanding and allowed the Witness children to exercise their religious liberty. Two boys who had been expelled from the nearby East Stroudsburg school for refusing to salute, attended Chestnuthill and lived with us. I had children scoff at me because I did not participate in the parties or other activities in school connected with any of the holidays, such as Easter or Christmas.

In one respect I realize that our family practice was not consistent with Society policy. This was the celebration of my birthday. Jehovah's Witnesses have taught for years that birthday celebrations were wrong. But from my experience it was obvious that the prohibition did not always apply to everyone. My father was congregational servant and in close contact with Society headquarters, yet I had a birthday cake and party each year all through my childhood until 1949, when I was in the ninth grade. This was long after the Society's denunciation of birthday observance. Bert Cummings of Bethel, who shared my birthdate, sent birthday cards, and Max Larson, factory manager, often sent a remembrance. People from Bethel were even at some of the birthday parties. And up until the time of my disfellowshiping in 1964, my mother usually sent me something near that date.

At the age of thirteen I realized that I wanted to dedicate my life to the service of God and do His will for the rest of my life. Therefore, in 1948 at a circuit assembly in Hazelton, Pennsylvania, my father baptized me, symbolizing this dedication. I graduated as valedictorian from high school at sixteen, completed a thirteen-month secretarial course at Churchman's Business College, and then worked for a year. One of my aspirations was to be a member of the Bethel Family. I learned from one of my friends at Bethel that one of the girls was leaving and that there would be an opening. I was told that if I were interested and made application, there was a good chance I would be accepted, because my family was well known. It was the Society's policy that girls would first work at the cannery on Staten Island for a summer. Those who would go to work at Bethel would be selected from the girls there. These girls were normally pioneers who had put in two or three years of service. In July, 1954, I went to a district assembly in Toronto and attended a meeting for persons interested in Bethel service. President Knorr was there and asked me, "Do you really want to come to Bethel to work? Do you realize that you will have to come to stay for three years?" "Yes," I replied. "Can you report on August 12?" he asked. I told him I was working and would have to give my employer a two-week notice, but that I could report by that date.

My thought at this time was that the Society was God's organization; there was no doubt about that. I wanted to serve Jehovah. If it required spending the rest of my life at Bethel, I was willing to do that. I was even willing to give up getting married and having children if that was what God wanted of me. If I should get married, I wanted my husband to be a circuit servant or other full-time worker.

My duty during the first eight months at Bethel was housekeeping in the Bethel home. Each girl had approximately twenty rooms to keep clean and the beds to make every day but Sunday. One day I was notified to report to Brother Larson at the factory to accept a new duty there. He informed me I would have a desk in the Correspondence Department. I would be responsible for opening mail from one section of the country and dispersing it to the proper departments in the factory. At times it was necessary to write letters, signing them with the "Watchtower Bible and Tract Society" rubber stamp and my desk code letters. I was very pleased to be able to serve Jehovah in this (I thought) responsible position. So when, after several months, I was told to report downstairs to the Magazine Department to work, I was crushed, for I considered this a demotion. I felt I had not been faithful in the assignment Jehovah had given me. Also I couldn't understand why my overseer, Brother Harley Miller, had not come to me and lovingly told me how I had proved unworthy. Because I had known Brother Larson, the factory servant, from childhood, I felt I could discuss the matter with him. He informed me that my removal was because of a facial expression I had made to Brother Miller which showed a lack of respect for him. I learned later that he had never wanted me in the Correspondence Department in the beginning and that this was a good excuse for my removal. This was my first experience at the hands of God's "loving" organization and I was shocked.

Often, problems between Society leadership and those under it would be brought into the dining hall. President Knorr used his position at the head of the table (with microphone) to castigate those with whom he was having differences. One such conflict was obvious between President Knorr and Colin

Quackenbush, who was editor of *Awake!* at the time. The outcome of this division was a number of tirades in the dining hall and the eventual ouster of Colin from his position as editor and also his removal from the Bethel speaker's staff. He was given hard manual labor in the factory. Later he left Bethel.

It was, and still is, a well-advertized fact that everyone at Bethel, including the president of the Watchtower Society, received only room and board and $14.00 a month. Yet, what is not explained is how the president is able to stretch this amount to maintain a Cadillac, travel the world, take people to the most expensive restaurants, and see Broadway shows. People actually donate to him personally and he uses his expense account to travel first class.

It was also obvious that there was a vast difference in living standards between the Knorr penthouse apartment on the tenth floor of Bethel and the normal lot of the Bethel worker. After I had been at Bethel for a few weeks I received an invitation to visit President Knorr and his wife on the tenth floor. His apartment was beautiful, with murals on the walls, private kitchen, television, and other comforts. In addition, the president had a Bethel brother who served him personally and also acted as a cook. I mention this information because people naively believe that the position of Watchtower leadership represents a sacrifice. What difference does it make if one officially receives only $14.00 a month when he can live like a king?

When I resigned from Bethel in 1958, after four years of service there, my fiancé Bill and I spoke to my parents about what we had observed at headquarters. I said that I could see none of the love which we were constantly talking about in the organization. They replied that we should exercise patience and that things would work out in time. I was just glad to get away from it all. Bill and I were married on Harvest Moon,

September, 1958, and lived happily next door to my parents until Bill was disfellowshiped on December 12, 1962.

A few things should be mentioned about Bill's disfellowshiping. When the letter came from the Society which requested Bill's presence at his hearing, he asked me to call as many members of the congregation as I could, and ask them to appear when his case was to be considered. The Society letter had stated that he could have witnesses in his behalf. But when several dozen people came, the district servant denied them admittance. He said that they could sit out in their cars until the questioning was finished. Because of the cold and snowy weather, Bill was able to persuade him to let the people wait in a back room of the building. It was not known by the district servant until the hearing was over, but the room in which the people waited did not have a door on it, and they heard the entire trial. He was angry because he had wanted to keep the whole thing quiet.

My father was very upset about Bill's disfellowshiping. He asked him, "What are you going to do about it?" Then he added, "You know you can't stay here any more. You have done enough damage already." My father said this because a number of people who had heard the proceedings of Bill's disfellowshiping trial were leaving the Kingdom Hall. When those who were not at the hearing heard that he was declared guilty of "apostasy," many called and came to ask about the reason for the charge.

One man who left the Kingdom Hall was Dawson Gillem, a longtime neighbor of my folks. After Bill was disfellowshiped, he called Bill and me over to his farm and offered to give it to us. He also offered us $2,500 to fix it up, requesting only that he be allowed to stay there as long as he lived. Dawson was able to stay away from the Kingdom Hall for several years until one summer when my dad refused to cut his grain until

97

he would associate again. Here is an example of a man who goes to the Kingdom Hall and is reckoned a Jehovah's Witness although he does not believe that the Society is God's organization.

Although I had not been disfellowshiped as yet, I agreed with the things that Bill had concluded by that time. Parents, relatives, and friends all put pressure on me to remain faithful to the organization and to save the family from certain destruction. Although I was not told to leave Bill, it was indicated that if I did I would be cared for. I couldn't leave my husband because I didn't really have any reason to reject the position which he took. I suspected many things were wrong with the doctrines we believed as Jehovah's Witnesses, but at this point I did not have much concrete evidence for this feeling. This would come at a later time.

After my father's ultimatum Bill called his Witness brother, Leo, in Santa Ana, California, and told him what had happened. He was a painting contractor and offered to give Bill a job and teach him the trade. Bill had no experience in painting, but he was willing to learn. With this hope of a new start, we loaded up our car and a U-haul trailer and with our three small children left for California. As we pulled away from the Kingdom Hall which I had known from childhood, I stated the feeling that was in my heart, "I never want to set foot in there again."

After we arrived in Santa Ana, we rented an apartment and Bill began his new job with his brother Leo. He learned quickly and in a few years was an apprenticeship instructor. It was after only a few discussions with Bill that Leo stopped his association with Jehovah's Witnesses. Leo was disgusted when others who were formerly at Watchtower headquarters privately told him that they also did not agree with the Society's ban on blood transfusion, yet they continued as Witnesses. "What hypocrites," he would say.

Leo's wife Phyllis also saw this hypocrisy and soon recognized Witness leaders to be false prophets, after finding out that they had erroneously announced the end of the world three times (1914, 1918, 1925). The incident which revealed to her how ridiculous the Society's position could be, occurred when at the suggestion of her veterinarian, she had a blood transfusion given to her poodle to prolong its life. She couldn't believe Bill when he told her that the Society would say she had violated God's law. At his urging she wrote the Society on the matter and the response she received informed her that she *had* done wrong. Phyllis thought that this was ridiculous. She wrote again and asked if her cat eating a mouse would also be a problem; was this too against God's law? She was told that she should keep the cat under restraint and be more careful in handling it. She thought to herself, "How many cats have I seen which have drained the blood of their mouse victim before eating it?" The Society's position had become a *reductio ad absurdum*.

After living in the apartment for eight months, we were able to buy the house in which we now live. God had blessed our step of faith.

In October, 1963, my parents came to visit us to see if I had changed my mind, or if they could help me to do so. They did not stay in our home, but stayed with Bill's aunt and uncle a few blocks away. By this time I had been able to sort out my thoughts more carefully, and the attempts of my parents to change my mind were unsuccessful. They left after this, and have not been in our home since. I was not disfellowshiped until later, however, when it became known that I had attended a talk which Bill gave on the Witnesses and blood transfusion at a neighborhood church.

I was visited first by the local congregational servant and a circuit servant, and then later by two sisters from the Kingdom Hall. When I was asked if I agreed with my husband, I stated that I did. A short time later I learned that I was going to be disfellowshiped without a trial by the judicial committee of the Kingdom Hall in Brodheadsville, Pennsylvania, where my father was congregational servant. I requested a local hearing, and the judicial committee in Santa Ana acted as a proxy for the one in Pennsylvania.

After a news article concerning my disfellowshiping appeared in the *Register* of August 7, 1964, a number of former Witnesses and members of various "Bible Student" groups contacted us. Through them we learned many things about the Society's past which we had not known. We also studied materials which presented the doctrines of Evangelical Christianity and the answers to the claims of the Jehovah's Witnesses. We were amazed to find out how badly we had been deceived as Witnesses. I came to realize that although as a Witness I had studied the Watchtower literature carefully, I really wasn't much of a student of the Bible. In fact, I had never really allowed myself to think through anything about the Bible on my own.

For about four years after leaving Pennsylvania I continued to correspond with my parents. Then my mother stopped writing, and she has not written since. I still write letters, but they are never answered. When we visit them now, we cannot even get into the house, but our children are allowed to visit. Two years ago when we visited the farm my mother met me at the door. I asked her, "Mother, what do you want me to do to restore our relationship again?" Her answer could be summarized in one sentence, "Come back to the organization." Materially, this would be a very advantageous thing to do, since my parents are wealthy. But Bill and I could never return to an organization and a system which are so obviously false.

As Bill expressed in his testimony, the Witness finds it very difficult to leave the movement, because he cannot see where he might go. He is looking for another organization to which he might give his allegiance. Where did I go? To the Bible, God's Word, and to Jesus Christ as my Savior. It took me a while to realize that my reliance for salvation was wholly on Him. No organization died for my salvation. This was a matter between Jesus Christ and me. I realized that he cared for *me!* I applied verses like John 3:16 personally: "For God so loved the world, that he gave his only begotten Son, that whosoever [Joan Cetnar] believeth in him should not perish, but have everlasting life." I would recommend that the person who leaves the Witnesses find a Bible-believing church where he might worship, grow spiritually, and fellowship with other Christians; he needs the contact.

I thank God for the way He has blessed our family and for the way He has met our needs: spiritual, physical, and material. I also thank Him that I am closer to Him now than I was ten years ago. A Christian's relationship with God is a vital, blessed, growing relationship. Praise Him!

**Walter and Carol Davis**

VIII

## I FOUND "THE TRUTH"—
## JESUS CHRIST

by

Walter Davis

I was born December 14, 1935, in Fort Worth, Texas, and have lived most of my life in or near San Bernardino, California. At the time I was first approached by the Jehovah's Witnesses, I was a member of the Reorganized Church of Jesus Christ of Latter Day Saints. I joined that church at the age of fourteen because of the influence of an aunt and some neighbors who were members. In my youthful enthusiasm and complete ignorance of what the Bible taught, I accepted as truth all the church's doctrines and practices, and I believed sincerely that it was *the one true* religion on the earth. To me Joseph Smith was a prophet of God called to restore the true church out of apostasy. I came to believe that his male descendants, as presidents of the church, were also prophets, seers, and revelators, and that *The Book of Mormon* and *Doctrine and Covenants* were equal to the Bible as scripture, and that continuous (modern day) inspired revelations were communicated through prophets.

My parents were nominal Christians of the Southern Baptist faith, and did not greatly oppose my joining the R.L.D.S. My mother's father, although he remained a Methodist, had read Judge Rutherford's books and had accepted his teachings as truth. As a result of her father's beliefs, my mother would always give the Jehovah's Witnesses a courteous reception when they called at the house. I have early childhood memories of listening to phonograph recordings of Judge Rutherford. Mother would frequently take Witness literature, but she did not believe what they taught. At first she accepted the R.L.D.S. teachings, but never was baptized in that church. I studied diligently, and my zeal was such that I was ordained to the office of deacon in the Aaronic Priesthood at age seventeen. At my ordination ceremony I was told (supposedly through prophecy) that I would become a "valiant warrior for the Lord in His Church."

A number of things occurred in 1953 which together resulted in my decision to leave the R.L.D.S. Church. My father was employed at this time as a union picket, and during labor union strikes I would frequently accompany him, often carrying a sign in front of retail stores. I recall very vividly my first personal encounter with a Jehovah's Witness while on picket duty in downtown Fontana, California. A friendly, well-dressed, middle-aged man holding *The Watchtower* and *Awake!* magazines, approached and began to witness to me on the street. I listened politely, but then told him that I wasn't interested in his religion since I believed that I already had the true one. He responded that if I had the truth, I should be sharing it and telling it to others, like Jehovah's Witnesses. He talked to me

103

for about one hour and challenged me to restudy the R.L.D.S. doctrines, for many contradicted the Bible. I took the magazines from him and purchased my first Watchtower Bible and Tract Society book, *What Has Religion Done for Mankind?* I took the book home, put it on the bookshelf, and forgot about it. My mother saw it, however, and she began to study it. Later she told me that if the book were true, then the R.L.D.S. faith was wrong.

The next time the Jehovah's Witnesses came to our home, Mother willingly took the literature they offered her. On their return call, she agreed to have a weekly Bible (book) study with them. She studied *Let God Be True* (2nd edition) as well as other Society publications. Because she worked odd hours as a nurse's aid, she frequently missed a study and was not able to attend the Kingdom Hall meetings every Sunday. As her study of the teachings of the Jehovah's Witnesses progressed, she began to share with me the "new truth" she was learning and to invite me to sit in on the studies. This only angered me, because I was a good deacon in the R.L.D.S. and was convinced that I already had the truth. By this time Mother had rejected my church's teachings and was constantly attempting to set me straight on doctrine. To silence her and to refute the Jehovah's Witnesses in her presence, I finally agreed to meet with them.

I sincerely believed that I could prove my "Mormon"[1] doctrines to be true and my mother's Jehovah's Witness beliefs to be false. Needless to say, meeting with the Jehovah's Witnesses to discuss my doctrines proved to be a disaster for my position, because I was ignorant of the Bible. I had been taught to support my church's teaching by using "proof texts."

---

1. The Reorganized Church of Jesus Christ of Latter Day Saints doesn't like the designation "Mormon," but I use it because we believed in *The Book of Mormon.*

Later I found that these were often out of context. This encounter with the Jehovah's Witnesses succeeded in planting doubts in my mind. I had been taught that the Bible supported "Mormon" doctrine; that, in fact, had been one of the main reasons for my joining the R.L.D.S. Church. I reasoned that if the Bible—the oldest and first of God's divine revelations—did not support the teachings of *The Book of Mormon* and *Doctrine and Covenants*, then these "latter-day scriptures" must be false. I carefully studied each Bible text used to support *The Book of Mormon*, and by God's leading I came to see that they were misinterpreted, taken out of context, and used in an erroneous manner.

I had set out to disprove the Jehovah's Witnesses, but in the process had proven my own church's teachings false. It was in December of 1953, as a junior in high school, that I left the R.L.D.S. Church. I attended my first Kingdom Hall meeting and shortly thereafter began to study the Witness books *Let God Be True* and *This Means Everlasting Life* with Witnesses Al and Betty Kusy in San Bernardino. I was seriously interested in learning the truth and earnestly studied for long hours every "truth" publication I could obtain.

The more I studied and learned about "The New World Society of Jehovah's Witnesses," the more convinced I became that they truly were Jehovah God's witnesses. The thing that impressed me most about the Witnesses was their rapid expansion as an international society of ministers of all races, nationalities, and languages. My former church was relatively small (only 125,000 members in less than two dozen countries), gaining about 5,000 new converts yearly, while the Jehovah's Witnesses were exploding in membership (over 500,000 when I joined) and adding tens of thousands of new members on a worldwide basis. I soon accepted all their doctrines. The belief that we were living in the last days since

105

1914 made a great impact upon my mind. The urgency to qualify as a minister of Jehovah and to share in preaching the "gospel of the kingdom" to the "other sheep" became the most important thing in life to me. I came to the point in my life where, in accordance with Society teaching, I dedicated myself to Jehovah God and vowed to be obedient to "the faithful and discreet slave" class in Brooklyn, New York.

In a public ceremony in Pomona, California, on June 6, 1954, I was baptized by water immersion to symbolize my dedication. Since Jehovah's Witnesses also consider one's baptism to be an ordination ceremony, I became an ordained minister. My conversion from "Mormonism" had created quite a sensation among the local Jehovah's Witness congregations, and I was "invited" to share my experience with the "brethren." However, I was shy and introverted as a youth and was always very nervous when speaking before an audience. Embarrassment and the fear of bungling in front of large crowds prompted me to try to keep from appearing. This was when I first became acquainted with the "strong arm tactics" of the Society.

The man with whom I had studied, Al Kusy, and my congregation servant told me in no uncertain terms that I would be expected to comply with this request of the circuit servant. To refuse to do so would be viewed as putting my "own selfish, individualistic interests" before those of the Society and would really amount to disobedience. I was to be exhibited as one who had tried to refute Witness "truth" and, having failed to do so, had become a Jehovah's Witness. As a member of the R.L.D.S. Church, I had been taught that we were not "Mormons," since people associated that term with polygamy and Brigham Young. Because there were many Mormons in Southern California, the Society obviously believed that by having me appear as a "Mormon" who had become a Jehovah's Witness, I might induce some L.D.S. people to convert.

My objections to appearing as a "Mormon" were rejected. I was told to submit because the Society considered the R.L.D.S. as "Mormons." This appearance would advance the theocratic interests; my experience would be shared with L.D.S. in hopes of inducing them to study with Jehovah's Witnesses. I finally agreed to give my testimony of how I had come out of "Mormonism." I, of course, had some mental reservations about the truthfulness of what I was doing. I gave my experience before 2,000 Jehovah's Witnesses at a circuit assembly, and later before 20,000 Jehovah's Witnesses at the 1954 district convention held at the Del Mar Racetrack. Afterwards I was applauded, congratulated, and told that my experience had greatly encouraged the brethren to witness to the Mormons with greater zeal.

My affiliation with the Witnesses had a mixed effect upon my family. My father, although an admitted backslider, had on several occasions with tear-filled eyes testified to me of his being "born again" as a boy at an old-fashioned revival meeting in Texas. I was emotionally moved while listening to Dad relate his experience of coming to know the Lord personally. He would tell me that the Jehovah's Witnesses were wrong and that I needed to be "born again" to be a real Christian. Although he couldn't fully explain their doctrines, he always exhorted me to become a Baptist, who, he claimed, preached the true gospel of Jesus Christ. As a Jehovah's Witness I would argue that only the 144,000 anointed ones would be "born again" at their physical death, when they would be changed to spirit creatures. My defense of the Watchtower teachings angered him and resulted in a break in our relations. Mother was later baptized into the Jehovah's Witnesses at their large district convention held in Wrigley Field, Los Angeles, in July, 1957. My younger brother Gary accepted many of their doctrines, although he was never baptized and did not join them. Later, while serving in the U.S. Navy, he accepted the Lord Jesus Christ. My relations with other relatives also became strained, if not hostile.

In my final year of high school, I decided to meet the Society's requirements for a pioneer. I had taken an academic major with plans for college after graduation. These plans were abandoned in accordance with Society instructions to "seek first the Kingdom rather than worldly higher education." Several of my teachers and my counselor pleaded with me to go on to college, but I turned a deaf ear to them. Pioneering, Gilead training, and eventually service as a foreign missionary had become my life goals. I worked for fifteen months in a box factory, saving money to purchase an automobile. During this time I was active in all phases of the field service.

By this time I had enrolled in the Theocratic Ministry School and was delivering short talks on subjects assigned by the "School servant." I took part in the program of the Service Meeting, which taught Jehovah's Witnesses how to engage in their ministry. I attended the Watchtower Study meeting where we received "new light" on the Scriptures, as well as the public talk every Sunday, which was mainly for instructing the new people of "good will." I soon qualified as a public representative of the Watchtower Bible and Tract Society and delivered my first public lecture in 1956. Afterwards, as part of the speaker exchange program, I gave discourses in a number of surrounding congregations. My father came to hear me give public talks; otherwise he would never attend.

Men who qualified to deliver public lectures as representatives of the Watchtower Bible and Tract Society had to use a Society-prepared outline on a subject chosen in Brooklyn. In preparing their lectures speakers could use only Watchtower publications or such other material officially approved. We could not use non-Society outlines, or religious publications of

108

non-Society scholars. I recall an instance where a lecturer quoted something on Bible numerics from Ivan Panin and encouraged the brethren to study Panin's books since "they contained much truth." He was disciplined by our congregation servant for advising the brethren to "feed at another spiritual table than Jehovah's table—The Watchtower."

I have a recollection of another occasion when I was personally disciplined for "getting out of line." My "sin" was delivering a talk on the Lord's Prayer at an area book study. I had used a previous *Watchtower* article setting forth the Society's views on Matthew chapters 5–7. I had tried to vary my topics when speaking at the area studies because we all had heard the same public lectures many times over at the Hall. I recall hearing frequent complaints, especially from new brethren, about how boring the same talks became after hearing them several times. What I had done was really not a violation of Society instructions. Our "servants" wanted us to give the same public talks at the smaller area study meetings. Because a number of people commented favorably on my speaking on various themes, some of the other speakers became jealous and complained to the local overseer. He called me in and warned me to follow his instructions. Only subjects of public lectures delivered in the Kingdom Hall were to be used at the local area talks once a month. Thereafter, I "theocratically" rehashed a public lecture at the area study speaking assignment.

I had held our congregation servant in high esteem when I first joined the Witnesses. But I was to learn that he had many weaknesses, among them a great fondness for strong drink. Many Jehovah's Witnesses manifested a strong appetite for alcoholic beverages; this always bothered me because I had been taught total abstinence by my parents and by my R.L.D.S. teachers. Drink was certainly a problem for my overseer, who worked for the railroad. After I left the Jehovah's

109

Witnesses a Christian employee on the railroad told me that he had once seen him so drunk on the job that he couldn't work. The problems he and his wife had with his mother were common knowledge among the congregation publishers. His wife made his mother move out of the house, and she was taken in by another Witness family. He and his step-daughter also had strained relations.

The Ministry School servant was a cold, aloof, yet domineering individual who alienated many "brethren" by his overly critical remarks and attitude. A couple that he and his wife had studied with and had brought into "the truth," left the organization after only six months. I called on this couple myself to try to win them back after the overseer had failed to do so. They said that it had become obvious to them that they were befriended as an inducement to get them to join the organization. Others in the local Hall had also been very cordial toward them until they were baptized. Then the situation changed. They were then told to think theocratically and not independently. The Ministry School servant and his wife ceased to socialize with them and became distant. They said this experience had opened their eyes to the real motives of these Witness "friends," and they felt that Jehovah's Witness "servants" were interested in new publishers only to the extent that they advanced theocratic interests. This couple left the congregation, and I later heard they had joined a Russellite sect.

It was obvious to me that our congregation servant retained his position because of his "theocratic obedience," rather than because of his Christian character. Shortly before I became a Jehovah's Witness in 1954, the San Bernardino congregation had been divided into two units. I was associated with the East Unit, which had a majority of white publishers, while the West Unit had a preponderance of black and Mexican

Witnesses. The Society has boasted much of the love and unity among Jehovah's Witnesses, and this claim, which I believed to be true, had helped draw me to it. I was to learn in reality that with many Jehovah's Witnesses this was not the case. The East Unit overseer would frequently refer to the West Unit as that "Congo" or "Ubangi" congregation and would state contemptuously that he didn't want any of those "ignorant blacks delivering lectures in our congregation." I once overheard a white brother remark about a black brother who was an accomplished speaker, "He may be a nigger, but he sure can talk!" Mexicans, who conversed in Spanish together in the presence of whites, were eyed with suspicion and were disliked by some white Witnesses.

After a few years of association with the so-called New World Society, I came to the realization that many people who were in it were really little different from those of the world. I had to admit to myself (I couldn't have to other Jehovah's Witnesses) that we were really no better or worse in our attitude, character, and life than any other group of religious people. The Society was continually exhorting us in the pages of *The Watchtower* and at assemblies to produce the fruit of the Spirit as found in Galatians 5:22-23. Yet the emphasis was on organizational thinking. Such thinking, we were told, would produce this fruit. We were not to be concerned with independently producing a Christian character, for this was viewed as selfish, dangerous, untheocratic thinking which would put us out of step with the victorious march of the Society into the New World.

I look back now and realize how this "theocratic" thinking often produced unhappy, miserable people. I recall a large German family of Witnesses whose father had died. The mother and her children were very active in the field ministry. Mrs. Kramer was the one who first studied with my mother, and it was with her older children that I first debated "Mormon" doctrine. An older son and two older daughters were local pioneers. Her son Don, a pioneer, once told me that his mother had caught him studying the old Society books written by "Pastor" Russell. Don said he had been comparing the differences between what Russell taught and what the Society then taught. This upset his mother so much that she took the books and burned them. This family was so maligned and ill-treated by the other Witnesses that the oldest son hated Jehovah's Witnesses, and the youngest son suffered a nervous and emotional breakdown. Several years after my mother and I had left the Society, she met Mrs. Kramer once on a downtown street. This poor old lady poured out her woes to my mother and concluded by saying, "We have been treated terribly by that bunch down at the Hall, but they will be judged at Armageddon. But they have the truth, Mrs. Davis, so come on back into the organization." Mother witnessed to her about faith in Christ as *The Truth*.

I recall meeting a Jewish Witness at a convention who pioneered with his wife. In talking to him about his discovering "the truth," I recall vividly something he said to me. He stated that he had been a baptized Jehovah's Witness for a year and a half before he really believed in Christ Jesus as the Messiah. Hearing this caused me to remember my dad's testimony of the necessity of being "born again" by accepting Jesus Christ as my Savior. Jesus had been little more to this Witness than a name in Watchtower publications. He said the name Jehovah meant more to him than the name Jesus Christ. This Jewish fellow and his Gentile wife were later sent to Israel as Watchtower missionaries. Most Jehovah's Witnesses referred to Jesus Christ as "the Savior," but rarely as "my Savior."

After meeting the Society's requirements for pioneering, I

bought a car and began to pioneer in my home congregation on November 1, 1956. I can honestly state that I did enjoy my pioneer experience as a Jehovah's Witness and do have some fond memories of it. My sorrow and regret is that I was not really preaching "The Truth"—Jesus Christ—and bringing people into a saving relationship with Him. I witnessed on the streets and from house to house, made back calls on literature placements, conducted book studies with people of "good-will," and delivered public lectures. By Society standards, I was a good Jehovah's Witness pioneer.

In January, 1957, at a circuit assembly in Victorville, California, I was introduced to an attractive college girl. I was told by some "sisters" in her congregation in Colton that Carol Jean Bourquein had just begun to study "the truth." Her mother, Ethel M. Waller, had studied with Dema White for several years and was now witnessing to her daughter daily. Carol had dated a Mormon fellow who had taken her to his church. Because she had some questions regarding both L.D.S. and Witness teaching, I was strongly encouraged to start a study with her. I called on her for the first time some time in February and soon began a regular study with her. I answered her questions about Mormonism, and she soon became a serious student of Jehovah's Witness doctrine. She was still in college at this time and soon began to witness to instructors and fellow students. Our friendship deepened and we began to date frequently. I greatly admired the way Carol was accepting the organization, although her questioning of certain teachings (e.g., the anointed class of 144,000) did bother me.

On April 22, 1957, another young pioneer—Bill Korinek— and I were reassigned by the Society to work with a small congregation in Riverton, Wyoming. Accepting this as Jehovah's will, Bill and I reluctantly said goodbye to our girlfriends,

113

relatives, and friends in San Bernardino. Bill was one of the first young fellows of my age that I had met among the Witnesses. We made a good team. He was of Czech-Austrian descent and had been raised as a Witness. He had turned down a full-tuition college scholarship in order to become a pioneer. I thought a lot of him, and the two of us became very close as a result of our pioneer experiences, but his stubbornness sometimes irritated me.

The publishers in the unassigned territory of Riverton-Lander, Wyoming, warmly welcomed us. I was greatly impressed with Wyoming's beautiful countryside and clear, blue skies. I threw myself energetically into the work of building up the small congregation there. Riverton was geographically in the largest circuit in the United States, yet it had the smallest number of publishers. My experiences there were many and varied. For relaxation I can recall on Saturday nights we would watch TV at the home of a more affluent brother. Frequently one of Billy Graham's crusades was televised. We would watch it and make sarcastic remarks about his being "an emotional, hell-fire-and-brimstone revivalist.'" I thought to myself that if Graham's preaching were true about the necessity of the "new birth," then we Witnesses were still in our sins.

Bill and I frequently discussed other religions and their teachings. I asked him once (after thinking about those people who went forward to make decisions for Christ at Graham's crusades), "Bill, do you ever think that we could be wrong in our religion?" I recall that he smiled and replied, "Yes, Walt, I do sometimes wonder. But if we're not right, then nobody is!" He was thoroughly brainwashed from childhood in the Society's doctrines. By contrast I had come in after the traumatic experience of proving "Mormonism" wrong. While I might have appeared outwardly dogmatic, the experience of

114

having once been proven wrong produced an uneasiness within me. By now I had experienced disillusionment about the character and attitude of many Witnesses, but I still rationalized that the things that made us Jehovah's true organization were our correct beliefs and practices.

Occasionally I met people at the door who invited me into their homes and after listening to my presentation they then told me of how Christ had saved them. They testified to me about the assurance the Holy Spirit had given them of their salvation and of the inner peace and joy they had in the Lord Jesus Christ. Of course, I tried to argue with them as a good Witness that they were wrong in their belief. I argued that one could not know definitely that he was saved until after Armageddon and the millennium were passed. I told them no one was saved by faith alone, but that good works and accurate knowledge were also essential to salvation. But sometimes at night, I lay on my bed, recalling the day's experiences, and the testimonies of these "born again" Christians with their "know so" salvation troubled me. I knew in my heart that I had no personal assurance of salvation based on a vital living relationship with Jesus Christ. I hoped I was saved thus far, but believed that I could lose it by unfaithfulness to the Society. I really didn't have the same peace, joy, and happiness that I saw radiating from the faces of these men and women who lovingly testified of their Lord Jesus Christ. They sometimes pleaded tearfully with me to confess myself a sinner and receive Jesus Christ as my own personal Savior. This only upset me, and in anger I rushed from their homes. But I believe now that the Holy Spirit was planting the good seed in my heart through the personal testimonies of these wonderful Christian people. I expected people at the doors to be hostile, or passively disinterested, or open to accept my "gospel." It came as something of a shock to meet people who believed so strongly in Christ that they would witness to me—a Jehovah's Witness.

I had read William J. Schnell's book, *Thirty Years a Watch Tower Slave*, while in California. I had agreed with his criticisms about the character and lives of many Witnesses, but felt he was just a disgruntled "evil slave." A. H. Macmillan's book, *Faith On the March*, succeeded in offsetting in my mind many of Schnell's criticisms of the inner workings of the Society. Still I believed that some of Schnell's statements were true and justified.

Bill and I returned to California for two weeks in the latter part of July, 1957, to visit our parents and to attend the large convention held in Wrigley Field. I dated Carol, visited relatives and friends, and really enjoyed my short visit.

We left San Bernardino on our return journey to Wyoming on the evening of July 31, 1957. A Jehovah's Witness woman, Marian McCarty, and her three children accompanied us on this trip. Bill, Marian, and I rotated driving, intending to drive day and night with only a few stops. We stopped for breakfast about 5:00 A.M., August 1, at St. George, Utah. As we were getting into the car after breakfast to resume our trip, something occurred which I now believe was the Lord's doing. Ordinarily I have a tendency towards motion sickness if I ride in the rear seat of an automobile, especially after a meal and on long trips. Normally I either drive or sit in the right front seat.

On this particular morning, Bill insisted that he was going to ride up front because he was tired of having to ride in the back seat with the three boys. Usually I would either have argued or refused to ride in the back seat after eating, but for some reason I just quietly agreed to do so. My life was spared as a result of this seemingly minor decision. Marian began to drive and about one hour later we had a serious wreck that completely demolished Bill's car. After driving a while, Marian had fallen asleep at the wheel, and the car swerved off the

116

highway onto the soft shoulder of the road. The jolting of the tires on the rough rocks awakened her. In her sleepy condition she saw a bridge ahead of us. Thinking she was stepping on the brakes, she actually floorboarded the accelerator and we hit the bridge traveling at approximately fifty miles per hour (according to the Utah Highway Patrol estimates).

Our car struck the bridge with such an impact that one of the metal support cables broke and rammed through the hood and dashboard. This cable jabbed into Bill's abdomen, breaking a number of ribs and seriously injuring his liver and other internal organs. Marian, thrown into the windshield, received several cuts and lacerations which disfigured her attractive face. Other than being shaken up and receiving a few minor cuts and bruises, the boys were really not hurt. Passing cars quickly stopped and several drivers rendered first-aid to us until the ambulance arrived. My fears were that Marian, who was bleeding from facial wounds, and Bill, who was softly moaning, would die before we could get them to the hospital. At first I thought my right arm was broken because it had an ugly gash. I recall thinking, "I must not have a blood transfusion."

We were rushed to the Iron County Hospital in Cedar City, Utah, where Marian and I were treated and released after a few days. Bill's injuries were very serious with much loss of blood due to internal hemorrhaging. In less than three weeks he had three major surgeries. He had refused all the doctors' requests to submit to blood transfusions and insisted on signing a paper forbidding them to give him blood. He was given blood substitute transfusions, but he grew progressively weaker as he continued to lose blood.

Bill's mother and his fiancée, Sandra Danchuck, came from California to be with him. His mother held Marian responsible for the accident and his subsequent death. She spoke bitterly

117

of Marian and wanted nothing to do with her. I recall the Mormon doctor pleading with Mrs. Korinek to agree to a blood transfusion for her son. She vehemently refused his request, stating, "I would rather see my boy dead and in the grave than see him violate Jehovah God's commandment against blood!" Bill finally died as a direct result of not receiving a transfusion. His doctor was visibly shaken over Bill's death and said that operating on him without a transfusion was like operating with one hand tied behind his back.[2]

---

2. In August, 1973, while on a vacation with my family, I stopped at the Zion Motel in Cedar City, Utah. We had a brief visit with the managers, Joe and Annie Lee Roberts, who had been very friendly and helpful to us all during our stay there in August, 1957. I had stayed in one of their motel rooms for about one-and-a-half weeks before returning to San Bernardino after the accident. They are Mormons and I had left Watchtower publications with them. During my brief stay there, I witnessed from house to house and on the street, placing a number of Society publications. I always enjoyed witnessing to Mormons as I knew their doctrines and how to refute them. Mrs. Roberts told me that she had vivid memories of our stay at their motel and of the events which related to the accident. She stated that on the day of the evening Bill died she had a long conversation with his mother. During their conversation, Sandra remained inside the room, listening to what was said. Mrs. Korinek was distraught and with much anguish said, "What shall I do? What do you think I should do, Mrs. Roberts?" Mrs. Roberts replied, "If it were my son, I would leave it up to the doctor to decide. He knows what's best." Then Mrs. Korinek said, "That's what I'm going to do. I'll tell the doctor to do what he thinks is best." Then Sandra rushed out of the room and said, "Oh, no, Mom! You can't go back on your word. You can't lose faith now. Bill wouldn't want the transfusion." Mrs. Roberts said that Sandra verbally browbeat Mrs. Korinek into submission to her will. Before this tirade, Mrs. Korinek had finally decided to permit Bill's doctor to give him a blood transfusion. I was amazed to hear this as I only knew of her refusal to allow it. Later that evening, after Bill's death, Mr. and Mrs. Roberts drove Sandra and Mrs. Korinek to the hospital. Upon seeing Sandra, Bill's doctor said to her, "Come here. I want you to see what you have done." He took Bill's lifeless hand and placed it in Sandra's hand. Mrs. Roberts stated that Bill's corpse was as white as a sheet

118

The automobile accident and Bill's death were very traumatic events in my life. I was so saddened over Bill's loss as a companion that I decided to return home rather than continue on to Wyoming. I requested and received from the Society a transfer of assignment back to the San Bernardino, California, East Unit. Bill's body was shipped by rail back to California and his funeral was held in a packed mortuary in San Bernardino. Although at times we had had heated arguments, I felt toward Bill as I did toward my own brother. I took his death hard and was in a confused mental state for weeks. Thoughts and questions about his death kept running through my mind.

I was able to rationalize Bill's death from lack of blood transfusions according to the Society's teachings. But questions kept plaguing me about the correctness of our position on this matter. I believed that Bill had maintained integrity and was in the grave awaiting a resurrection after Armageddon in God's new world. But, what if blood transfusions were not really considered by God to be a feeding on blood? What if the scriptures used by the Society were misinterpreted and used out of context? As I carefully reread Genesis 9:3-5, Leviticus 17:14, Acts 15:28, 29, and other scriptures which the Society said prohibited blood transfusions, it seemed more to me that they applied to the ancient religious custom of eating flesh and blood as a part of a worship ceremony. They really did not seem to apply to the modern lifesaving medical practice of transfusing blood from one person to another.

---

from loss of blood. Mrs. Korinek suffered great anguish over the loss of her son. Sandra maintained her composure in the presence of others, but once while alone with me she completely broke down emotionally. She sobbed, "Why did Bill have to die? Why did Jehovah have to take him from me?" At that time, I must confess, I really couldn't comfort her very much.

Recalling the experience of discovering how erroneous the R.L.D.S. Church was in trying to prove *The Book of Mormon* from the Bible, I wondered if the same twisting of Scripture was being done by the Society. I was greatly perplexed about this, and talking to the brothers about this teaching and Bill's death only made me more confused. Finally, I forced myself to dismiss from my mind all these doubts and questions about the Society. After all, I felt, they were God's anointed servants. They just could not be wrong. And if they were wrong, where would I go? What would I do? I decided to remain a faithful Witness and to stay active in the New World Society.

I redoubled my field service activity in the pioneer work in September and October, 1957, trying to drown my misgivings and doubtings by theocratic activities. Carol and I became engaged at this time. I made plans to discontinue the pioneer service for a while, until Carol could qualify, and then resume pioneering together as husband and wife. We both planned to work, save our money to buy a house trailer and better car, and then join the hundreds of other couples pioneering in unassigned territory. As we discussed our plans for the future, pioneering and eventual foreign missionary work became our common goal. She had made good progress in studying and was active in all phases of the field service. I requested the Society to remove my name temporarily from the pioneer list and this was done on November 1, 1957. Carol and her mother were baptized at the circuit assembly in Riverside, California, on November 9, 1957. They became enthusiastic members of the Colton Congregation and witnessed much to their non-member relatives.

During my last two months of pioneer activity, I believe now that the Holy Spirit began to lead me step-by-step to that momentous day of decision—the day my spiritual eyes were opened to my lost, sinful condition as a theocratic slave, the day of my rebirth into God's kingdom. It seemed that in my feverish activity to forget Bill's death, I was meeting daily, or several times a week, more "born again" Christians at the door. They would tell me of their joy in knowing the Lord Jesus Christ as their personal Savior and Lord of their lives. Of course, I would tell them that they were wrong and doomed for destruction at Armageddon. We would have long discussions about the plan of salvation and would compare and argue many Scripture texts.

The Holy Spirit led me to the home of an elderly man with whom I had a memorable discussion; its details are clear in my mind even after nearly sixteen years. This man's father had been one of C. T. Russell's early converts in Kentucky around the turn of the century. His father had been a colporteur for the "Millennial Dawn Bible Students," as Jehovah's Witnesses were called then. He had been a faithful Russellite, but had come to see the errors in the Society, and after receiving Christ and the "new birth" had left it. After leaving, he traveled widely, calling on those with whom he had left Russell's books, and before he died he was successful in leading many to a saving knowledge of Jesus Christ.

On his death bed, this ex-Russellite had charged his son to continue to expose the errors of Pastor C. T. Russell and to present Christ to those ensnared in Russell's teachings. The son had remained faithful to the promise made to his dying father. He presented Jesus Christ to me as the One who is "the Way, the Truth, and the Life" (John 14:6). I told him that I had been a "Mormon" who had found the truth in Jehovah's Witnesses. He replied that I had not helped myself one bit, since no one comes to the Father except through Jesus Christ. I told him that I received "light" through *The Watchtower* magazines. He said the only way one could receive light from *The Watchtower* magazine was to set fire to it. Not

121

to be outdone, I argued with him for some time, attempting to prove that the Bible teaches one is saved by faith plus study, witnessing, endurance, obedience, and good works. He showed me how each text we used as Witnesses was taken out of context or misinterpreted. I wouldn't admit this to him, of course, and finally seeing that I was getting nowhere, angrily called him "an old goat," and left his house. His last words were that he loved me and would be praying that I would come to Christ. My experience with this elderly man remained with me and in the days following, I thought many times about his witness to me.

During this same period of time, I happened to call at the home of the pastor of the San Bernardino Community Church. He invited me in, and we discussed the Trinity and the deity of Jesus Christ. He shared with me his moving testimony of having been saved by personal faith in Jesus Christ from a life of drunkenness. Christ had cleaned up his life, sustained him in his studies at Biola College, and after graduation had called him into the ministry. As a gospel minister he was earning much less than he had formerly earned as a businessman. He said the Society's indictment of clergymen as being money hungry might apply to some liberal, modernist churchmen who preached the "social gospel," but it did not apply to the average, struggling pastor of an evangelical, fundamentalist church who truly preached the gospel.

We discussed at length his criticisms of the renderings of the Greek in the New World Translation of the Society. I recall how uncomfortable I became as I listened to this dedicated Christian pastor refute every point I made in trying to defend the Society's mistranslations. As I look back now, I can see how ridiculous, if not humorous, I must have appeared to this pastor as I argued with him about Hebrew and Greek. I was totally ignorant of these languages and of the disciplines of exegesis and hermeneutics. This kind Christian man never ridiculed me, but lovingly yet firmly showed me that if the Witnesses insisted on the New World Translation of John 1:1 and other texts, then we were polytheists and should not call ourselves Christians. Up until this time, except for the policy on blood transfusions, I had never seriously questioned the New World Translation and the Society's doctrines. He gave me Dr. Bruce M. Metzger's pamphlet, *The Jehovah's Witnesses and Jesus Christ*, for further study on the doctrines we had discussed.

Reading this pamphlet and thinking of my frequent experiences with "saved, born again" Christians motivated me to begin to study the Bible more seriously. Until now, most of my Bible reading had been done in conjunction with studying Watchtower literature. Now I began to study and meditate prayerfully on the Scriptures themselves. I cautiously shared with Carol some of the experiences I was having with Christians I had met. In her zeal as a newly baptized Witness, she dismissed them as religionists who were completely wrong. But I could no longer dismiss them so lightly.

After I stopped pioneering, I remained active in the field ministry, but my heart was no longer in it. I continued to attend the meetings and to give talks, but I was losing my zeal at the very time my future wife was becoming increasingly more zealous. My whole life was centered around the Society. I had always tried to be a good, faithful Jehovah's Witness. I had made mistakes and had sinned, but I had always remained theocratic in my allegiance. Doubts about the Society's teachings and practices bothered me, and I knew that I couldn't continue indefinitely in this mental state. I did not want to leave the Society, but I did decide that at all costs I was going to "let God be true" in my life (Rom. 3:3-4). I reasoned that if our faith as Witnesses was true, and based on the Bible, then honest and critical searching wouldn't disprove it.

As a pioneer, I had challenged hundreds of people to put their religion to the test. In the Foreword to *Make Sure of All Things* (p. 5), the Society encouraged us to study the "highest authority . . . the Holy Bible, Jehovah's Word." Now after having associated with the Society for four years, I was going to put it to the test of God's Word. The same publication stated:

> But Jehovah's advice goes even farther. The book of highest authority does not ask us to accept just one statement of truth, and that blindly; but rather God's prophet says: "Come now, and let us reason together, saith Jehovah."

This is what I resolved to do. I had been wrong before in my "Mormon" religion. Had I been misled and deceived a second time by the Watchtower Society?

One day I went into the Bible Book Store in San Bernardino and there met Pastor Robert Purcell, an ordained Southern Baptist minister. We struck up a conversation on the Scriptures and I soon introduced myself as a Jehovah's Witness who was sincerely searching for the truth of God's Word. Again I was to hear that Jesus Christ was "the Way, the Truth, and the Life." This time I didn't argue, but said that if I were wrong in my religion and Jesus were "the Truth," then I wanted Him. I refused to surrender my life to Jesus then, because I first wanted to get straight doctrinally. Bob encouraged me to purchase the book, *Jehovah of The Watchtower*, by Walter R. Martin and Norman H. Klann. It was an exposé of the history, doctrines, and anti-biblical teachings of Jehovah's Witnesses. I began to study it carefully along with the Bible. This book was used of God to open my eyes to the "pseudo-scholarship" of the Society. I had thought previously that its men were the greatest biblical scholars in the world.

124

Now, whenever I had questions that I wanted more information on, I would ask *both* the "mature brothers" in my congregation and the Rev. Bob Purcell. The conflicting answers I received from them only drove me to the Bible that much more. Throughout this time of searching I had the faith that Jehovah would lead me out of my perplexity into the real truth.

Carol and I were married in the Colton Kingdom Hall on December 28, 1957. John Stippich, a personal friend and former Bethelite, performed the ceremony. He had once told me that our Society's president, Nathan Homer Knorr, had it made if any man ever did. He lived in penthouse luxury compared to the others at Bethel. According to John, Knorr had only the finest and best of anything and everything he wanted. John told me there were things he had learned and seen back at Bethel that would shake the faith of the average brother in the Society if he knew about them. He would never tell me what these were, other than to say that the directors of the Society lived much better than the other brothers there. I recall his telling me once that, while he was at Bethel, one of the brothers (one of Knorr's favorites) had run away from Bethel and "joined up with Billy Graham" after writing Knorr a letter in which he denounced the Society.

I tried to share my doubts about the Society with Carol after our marriage. I challenged her with the statement that if the Society were wrong in its teaching about God, then it would be wrong in other doctrines. It took much persuasion on my part to get her to agree to restudy our doctrine about the Godhead. We would study the Scriptures with both Society and non-Society books. We began to listen to religious radio and TV broadcasts such as Dr. DeHaan's "The Radio Bible Class," Charles E. Fuller's "Old Fashioned Revival Hour," Billy Graham's "Hour of Decision," and Mike Perl's "The Hebrew-Christian Witness." I also met with Bob Purcell frequently

125

to discuss the deity of Christ, the deity and personality of the Holy Spirit, and other subjects.

After January 1, 1958, Carol and I were associated with the West Unit in San Bernardino. I was appointed area study servant, but resigned after only two months. The Holy Spirit, I believe, was leading me to question certain Society practices and teachings more openly with the congregation servants. When I disagreed with what they said, I told them so. My boldness angered them, and I was told that I had better be careful about questioning the Society and its teachings. Sometimes a week went by without my engaging in even an hour of field service activity, and I began to miss some meetings; Carol continued to go without me.

About April 1, 1958, I finally accepted the truth of the scriptural teaching on the Trinity. My Bible studies with the Rev. Bob Purcell and in numerous books such as *Jehovah of The Watchtower* had convinced me that the Bible taught that Jesus Christ claimed to be and is God, and that the Holy Spirit is a Person and is God. Bob was glad to hear of my acceptance of this scriptural teaching, but when Carol learned of it she was very upset. We had some serious arguments over biblical teaching. Her mother and others encouraged her to leave me and for a while I really didn't know if our marriage would last.

In the latter part of April, 1958, a "Spiritual Life" conference was held at Faith Bible Church, San Bernardino. I attended on Wednesday night and heard Dr. John Walvoord, president of Dallas Theological Seminary, speak on the "Fruit of the Holy Spirit." It was just like water to a thirsty man. After the meeting, I discussed the subject with him and even argued with him about some Society teachings that I still believed. He asked me if I had received the new birth. When I replied no, he told me that, spiritually, I was putting the cart before the horse. He told me, quoting I Corinthians 2:14, that I as a "natural man" could not understand or receive the things of the Spirit of God, for they are hidden from one who is spiritually dead and can only be "spiritually discerned." Dr. Walvoord said that I had to be "born again"; otherwise, I would never "see" or enter the kingdom of God. Quoting John 14: 16, 17, 26; 16:7-11, 13-15, he showed me that after I received the new birth the Holy Spirit would "guide me into all truth."

I returned the next night to hear Dr. Dwight J. Pentecost preach on "The Sin Against the Holy Spirit." This message was the proverbial straw that broke the camel's back. As I sat in the pew I realized that I had reached a crisis point in my life. I knew that if I walked out of church that night without accepting Christ, I would truly be sinning against the Holy Spirit. Yet I refused to go forward when the invitation was given. The final hymn was sung and the service was dismissed after prayer. Words cannot adequately describe my emotions during those next few minutes. I believe I felt about as close as possible to experiencing a "hell on earth." All of my past experiences as a Jehovah's Witness flashed through my mind. To do what I knew I had to do might cost me nearly everything. Carol might leave me. My Witness friends would renounce me. All my efforts and accomplishments as a Witness would be for nothing. My own mother might turn against me. But I prayed to my heavenly Father to give me the courage to do what was right. I saw Bob Purcell and told him with tears in my eyes, "Bob, I can't leave here tonight without accepting Jesus as my Savior." I simply could no longer postpone this decision.

The two of us went into a prayer room, got on our knees, and Bob prayed first, thanking the Lord for my decision. Then I prayed earnestly, confessing myself to be a self-righteous, religious sinner. I asked God to forgive all my sins. I asked the Lord Jesus to come into my heart and life. By faith I claimed the precious promises of the Word of God as my own. I arose a new man in Jesus Christ, filled with peace and joy for the first time in my life. I felt as if a mountain had been lifted from my shoulders.

When I returned home that night I told my wife of my decision and of my joy in the Lord. I had such a feeling of liberty. I told her that I was now free of the chains of Watchtower slavery. Regardless of what happened, I wanted nothing more to do with the Society. I really didn't know what her reaction was going to be. I was surprised and greatly relieved when I heard it. She said that she respected my decision to accept Christ as my Savior. (She had done this as a child in the Christian Church.) It was difficult for her to understand why I had decided to leave the Society and to see why I could not be "born again" and yet remain a Jehovah's Witness. She and her mother had once believed they were "born again" and still they had come into "the truth." I told her that they had been deceived.

In the days that followed, the Bible truly became a new book for me. I put aside all Watchtower literature and studied only God's Word. Christ's promise of spiritual guidance in John 16:13 became a living reality for me; Scripture seemed almost to jump from the pages as I read it. I was like a starving man sitting down to a feast. I began to attend church regularly, sometimes accompanied by Carol. She quickly began to understand the truths of God's Word as we studied and prayed together. It took a call from the unit servant and his assistant to open her eyes to the truth about the Society.

These two "brothers" began by questioning me about my absences at the meetings and my lack of field service activity. When I began to testify about my salvation experience and my

128

acceptance of Jesus Christ as Jehovah God in the flesh, they became very angry and called me an "evil slave." I remained calm and continued to witness to them about Jesus Christ. I shared with them Scripture verses proving that Christ is God, that He provided a completed salvation at Calvary, that He arose, ascended, and will return in His physical body, that the Holy Spirit is a Person and is God. They tried to refute these scriptural truths, but could not do so. Carol stood by, observing all that was taking place during this confrontation with the servants. They tried to out-talk me, but I would not let them do so. Then they tried jumping from subject to subject to try to save face in front of Carol. I kept them on the subject of the Godhead. Finally the congregation servant yelled at me, "You think you know more than the Society, don't you?" I replied, "Yes, I do believe that I know more about the Holy Scriptures than the Watchtower Society, since I have the Holy Spirit within me." This reply made them so angry that they began to defame my character and service. They claimed that I had never really been a good Witness, that I had given poor lectures and talks, was lazy, and had been a poor pioneer.[3] Yet I had been recognized in San Bernardino as a model of what a Society publisher and pioneer should be. Many Witnesses had told Carol how fortunate she was to be marrying such a fine, theocratic young man. Then Carol came to my defense and said they were lying in the things they were saying about me. She told them that she had been pleased to see them come at first, because she had hoped that they would lovingly show me my error and thus be able to reclaim me for the

---

3. This attack by my former "brethren" was not in agreement with the letter which I received from the Watchtower Society, dated February 21, 1959, which stated: "The quality and quantity of your workmanship is still remembered and appreciated. For that reason we are sending you this letter."

129

Society. Their hateful attitude and slanderous remarks had only demonstrated to her that they were not Christians and that I was a true Christian.

Carol ceased to associate with the Jehovah's Witnesses after that and continued to grow spiritually as we prayed, studied the Bible, and attended a gospel-preaching church. After I witnessed to my mother, she too left the Society; my brother also saw the error in their teaching. My parents later became members of a Baptist church associated with the Southern Baptist Convention. Carol's mother remained an active Witness for a year after we left the Society. We had some heated discussions with her on various subjects. She thought I was deceived and had misled her daughter. We continued to witness to her about our faith in Jesus Christ and "the faith which was once delivered unto the saints" (Jude 3). Her further doctrinal discussions with Carol were a violation of Society teaching against associating with an "evil slave." Ethel felt that the Society had no right to prohibit her from such contact with her own child. During this time she read a book on the great doctrines of salvation. She relates how she would pick up the book, read a few pages, get upset by what she read, put the book away, and later repeat the process. However, she slowly read through it and learned much truth from the Scriptures. She developed doubts concerning some of the teachings of the Society, such as the identification of the 144,000 as the only ones going to heaven and the view that the "anointed class" are the "angels" who do the preaching in the book of Revelation.

The area service center meeting one morning brought the crisis brewing in Ethel's life to a climax. The Bible text for discussion that day before going into field service was John 3:16. Ethel was shocked to hear that Jesus did not die to save the world of sinful men, but rather that He died for the

"New World Society of Jehovah's Witnesses." She could not accept this interpretation of a much-loved Bible text which plainly states that Christ died that "whosoever believeth in him should not perish, but have everlasting life."

Ethel phoned Dema White, the Witness who had brought her into "the truth," and informed her that she was leaving the organization. She ceased all activity with the Witnesses in Colton, and returned to her previous faith in Christianity. Her husband—who had never been baptized—ceased to believe their teachings after she showed him some of their errors. She was disfellowshiped later for refusing to appear before a disfellowshiping committee. She is now an active member of the Colton Community Church.

Since we left the organization, the Jehovah's Witnesses will not speak to us or even call at our home to witness. We are not certain whether we were ever disfellowshiped from the Society, because we never received any letters notifying us of such an action. We were never told to make the customary appearance before a disfellowshiping committee for a hearing. As far as we are concerned, it really makes no difference, since we know that we definitely resigned or voluntarily left the Society. We have no desire ever to return, for we have been delivered from the darkness of spiritual blindness and received God's glorious light (II Cor. 4:3-4). Our testimony is the same as Paul's in II Corinthians 4:6, "For God, who commanded the light to shine out of darkness, hath shined in our hearts, to give the light of the knowledge of the glory of God in the face of Jesus Christ."

While I was a "Jehovah's Witness," my life was characterized by "good works" in order to attain a right standing with God. Salvation was the goal toward which I was earnestly working. As one of the "earthly class" of "other sheep," I

131

hoped to maintain a record of personal integrity, thus vindicating Jehovah's name by my life. Many good works were essential to gain salvation in the paradise earth after Armageddon. I never had any assurance of my salvation; it was something to be obtained by right conduct and good works as a theocratic slave. In spite of all my efforts I did not have a personal relationship with the Lord Jesus Christ. If a Witness does not maintain a faithful course of integrity, he loses his chance of gaining everlasting life. As a Witness I recall hearing about people of whom it was said, "Since he left the Society, he will be slain at Armageddon and he has lost all hope of eternal life." This teaching applied even to the "heavenly class" of 144,000. The Witnesses' plan of salvation is based primarily on one's personal good works. Each Witness is working his way to everlasting life and cannot know that he is saved.

Since leaving the Watchtower Society, I have been led to reach Witnesses for Christ. The number has not been large, but there have been some who have come to a saving knowledge of Jesus Christ through my testimony. I have spoken in a number of evangelical churches to help other Christians better understand the Witnesses. Several people studying with Witnesses and thinking about joining the Society have been reclaimed from error and pointed to Christ. I do not hate Jehovah's Witnesses. As my former brethren, I love them. Using the words of Paul's desire for Israel in Romans 10:1-3, I can truthfully say,

> Brethren, my heart's desire and prayer to God for [Jehovah's Witnesses] is, that they might be saved. For I bear them record that they have a zeal of God, but not according to knowledge. For they, being ignorant of God's righteousness, and going about to establish their own righteousness, have not submitted themselves unto the righteousness of God.

As a Christian now for the past seventeen years, my life has

132

been characterized by a deep, abiding faith in Jesus Christ as my personal Savior-God. I have a personal relationship with Jesus Christ now; this is the most wonderful fact of my life. I abide in Jesus and He abides in me (John 15:4-5). I would challenge any Jehovah's Witness who might read my testimony to follow my course. Leave Watchtower slavery. Become a new person in Jesus Christ through the "new birth." The transformed life of a child of God, born of the Holy Spirit, is one of freedom, joy, and peace. My wife, son, and I are practicing Christians and are active members of the First Baptist Church of San Bernardino. I am presently on the Board of Deacons, chairman of the Evangelism Committee, and a discussion leader in Bible Study Fellowship. We share our faith in Jesus Christ in the power of the Holy Spirit and leave the results to God.

You who are still shackled by the chains of Watchtower slavery, prayerfully read these words. Jehovah God loves you with a greater love than the Society could ever describe (John 3:16; 10:10; Rom. 5:6-8). You are just a religious sinner like Saul of Tarsus, seeking to establish your own righteousness by good works (Rom. 3:23; 6:23). You can come to God only through Jesus Christ. He alone is Jehovah's only provision for man's sin (Rom. 5:8; I Cor. 15:3-6; John 14:6). You need individually to receive the Lord Jesus Christ as your Savior and Lord (John 1:12; Eph. 2:8-9; Rev. 3:20). After you have received the new birth (John 3:3, 5-7) by personal faith in Jesus Christ, you can know that you have everlasting life as a present possession (I John 5:11-13). This is the most precious verse of assurance to me and was a great comfort to me after I left the Society.

Our new life in Christ is received and lived by faith, not by emotion or mere knowledge. As Paul states, "the just shall live by faith" (Rom. 1:17). Our assurance of eternal life in

133

Jesus Christ is based upon the authority of God's Word (I John 5:9-13), the witness of the Holy Spirit within us (Rom. 8:16), and our transformed lives after we receive Christ (John 2:3-6). As a member of the Body of Christ (I Cor. 12:1-27), which is not divided, I share the one hope of all true Christians—to be with Christ in heaven (John 14:1-3). Christians, according to Paul in Ephesians 4:4-6, are called to only one hope, not two as the Watchtower Society teaches. There are no earthly class and heavenly class distinctions among Christians; we are all one flock in Christ (John 10:16).

For the past seventeen years I have been a witness for Jesus Christ. I never really knew or experienced the love of my heavenly Father until Jesus revealed Him to me, something the Society never did (Matt. 11:25-27). The heavy yoke of Watchtower religion has been replaced by the one described in Matthew 11:28-30. Although my former "theocratic" friends in the Watchtower Society have nothing to do with me now, I can say with Paul:

> But what things were gain to me, those I counted loss for Christ. Yea doubtless, and I count all things but loss for the excellency of the knowledge of Christ Jesus, my Lord; for whom I have suffered the loss of all things, and do count them but [refuse], that I may win Christ, and be found in Him not having mine own righteousness . . . but that which is found through the faith of Christ, the righteousness which is of God by faith: that I may know him, and the power of his resurrection, and the fellowship of his sufferings . . . [Phil. 3:7-10].

In recording this story of how I came to leave the Jehovah's Witnesses, I have not sought any personal glory or fame (Gal. 6:14). I conclude my testimony with a prayer to our Father in heaven that He might bless this account of my life experiences to the exaltation of Jesus Christ. May the reader join the writer of these lines in praising Him, whom

God also hath exalted . . . , and given him a name which is above every name: that at the name of Jesus every knee should bow, of things in heaven, and things in earth, and things under the earth; and that every tongue should confess that Jesus Christ is Lord, to the glory of God the Father [Phil. 2:9-11].

If the reader of this testimony is a misnamed "Jehovah's Witness," I invite you to accept my Lord Jesus as your Savior. Renounce the errors of the Watchtower Society. Stop trusting in your religious good works. Continuing to place your faith in the Society will only earn for you some day the Savior's words, "I never knew you: depart from me, ye that work iniquity" (Matt. 7:23). If you will call upon the Lord Jesus Christ as a religious sinner, He will forgive you all your sins (John 14:14). Ask the Lord Jesus Christ to save you and He will do so (Rom. 10:11, 13). Your transformed life as a new believer in Jesus Christ will be the out-living of the in-living Savior. With Paul you will then be able to say: "I am crucified with Christ: nevertheless I live; yet not I, but Christ liveth in me: and the life which I now live in the flesh I live by the faith of the Son of God, who loved me, and gave himself for me" (Gal. 2:20).

"The Solid Rock"

My hope is built on nothing less
    Than Jesus' blood and righteousness;
I dare not trust the sweetest frame,
    But wholly lean on Jesus' name.
On Christ, the solid Rock I stand;
    All other ground is sinking sand.

## IX

## THE JEHOVAH'S WITNESSES—A NON-PROPHET ORGANIZATION

Thousands of people have left the Jehovah's Witnesses because they became convinced that this organization, which claims to be Jehovah's "prophet," is in reality a non-prophet organization. An examination of many of the publications of the Watchtower Society in the light of history and such Bible passages as Deuteronomy 18:20-22 and Ezekiel 13:1-3 leads to the conclusion that this Society is a *false* prophet.

### The Claims of the Jehovah's Witnesses

The Jehovah's Witnesses claim that "they represent Jehovah" and are "Jehovah's earthly organization." Several statements from the April 1, 1972, *Watchtower* article, "They Shall Know that A Prophet was Among Them," are sufficient to clearly establish the Witnesses' claim to being a "prophet." This article explains that men can learn about God and what He expects of them in three ways: (1) by His creation, (2) through the Bible, and (3) "through his representatives." In ancient times God sent prophets who "foretold things to come" and who "served the people by telling them of God's will for them at that time, often also warning them of dangers and calamities." People today still have the testimonies of creation and

> the Bible, but it is little read or understood. So, does Jehovah have a prophet to help them, to warn them of dangers and to declare things to come?
>
> These questions can be answered in the affirmative. Who is this prophet? . . .

136

... This "prophet" was not one man, but was a body of men and women. It was the small group of footstep followers of Jesus Christ, known at that time as International Bible Students. Today they are known as Jehovah's Christian witnesses. . . .[1]

How long has God used the Watch Tower Bible and Tract Society and *The Watchtower* (current title) as His channel of communication? *The Finished Mystery,* published in 1917, quotes a *Watch Tower* issue of the same year:

"The WATCH TOWER BIBLE AND TRACT SOCIETY is the greatest corporation in the world, because from the time of its organization [1884] until now the Lord has used it as His channel through which to make known the Glad Tidings."[2]

In the first volume of J. F. Rutherford's book *Light,* published in 1930, it is claimed that since 1879 *The Watchtower* "has been the means of communicating truth to those who love the Lord. All those who love God supremely believe that *The Watch Tower* was started and has been maintained by his power and grace."[3]

While the Jehovah's Witnesses today stress "progressive" light to escape past errors and reversals of prophetic interpretation, it is obvious that they have claimed that since their inception the Society and *The Watchtower* magazine have been used as God's channel. Therefore, all Society publications must be included in assessing Witness claims to being God's channel of spiritual truth—His "prophet."

## The Tests of a Prophet

The Witnesses' *Aid to Bible Understanding* presents three

---

1. *The Watchtower,* July 1, 1973, p. 401; April 1, 1972, p. 197.
2. *The Watch Tower,* 1917, p. 22, quoted in *The Finished Mystery,* p. 144.
3. (Brooklyn: Watch Tower Bible and Tract Society), p. 12.

137

essential tests for identifying a true prophet of God as set forth by Moses:

> . . . the true prophet would speak in Jehovah's name; the things foretold would come to pass (Deut. 18:20-22); and his prophesyings must promote true worship, being in harmony with God's revealed word and commandments (Deut. 13:1-4). . . .[4]

It has already been established that the Witnesses claim to "represent Jehovah" and to be His "prophet" organization. Having taken the authority of speaking for Jehovah God, the Witnesses must be examined by the further tests of Scripture to determine whether their claim is valid. The April 1, 1972, *Watchtower* article cited above goes right to the heart of the matter when it states: "Of course, it is easy to say that this group acts as a 'prophet' of God. It is another thing to prove it. The only way that this can be done is to review the record. What does it show?"[5] The article proceeds to "review the record" by presenting the Witnesses' account of how they have functioned as the "prophet" of God. To anyone outside their organization this review proves nothing.

A more objective test is found in the application of the second identifying mark of a true prophet of God as stated in Deuteronomy 18:22:

> When the prophet speaks in the name of Jehovah and the word does not occur or come true, that is the word that Jehovah did not speak. With presumptuousness the prophet spoke it. You must not get frightened at him [NWT].

This test of one who claims to be a prophet is clear—when the true prophet speaks concerning future events, they *must*

---

4. (Brooklyn: Watchtower Bible and Tract Society of New York, Inc., 1971), p. 1348.
5. P. 197.

come to pass. The failure of fulfillment identifies the prophet as presumptuous—a false prophet.

What kind of "prophet" has been revealed over the years in the publications of the Watchtower Society?

## The Watchtower "Prophet" Tested

With a few exceptions the following statements are taken from the publications of the Watchtower Bible and Tract Society and they are presented chronologically. Additional statements for other years could be cited, but those which have been used should be sufficient to establish the fact that the Watchtower "prophet" has failed the biblical test of Deuteronomy 18:22.

### 1886–1899

The January, 1886, *Zion's Watch Tower* began with the observation:

> The outlook at the opening of the New Year has some very encouraging features. The outward evidences are that the marshalling of the hosts for the battle of the great day of God Almighty, is in progress while the skirmishing is commencing.
>
> .   .   .   .   .   .   .   .   .   .   .   .
>
> . . . The *time* is come for Messiah to take the dominion of earth and to overthrow the oppressors and corrupters of the earth, (Rev. 19:15 and 11:17, 18) preparatory to the establishment of everlasting peace upon the only firm foundation of righteousness and truth.[6]

In the 1889 publication, *The Time Is at Hand*, the pre-1914 interpretation of prophecy is set forth:

> Be not surprised, then, when in subsequent chapters we present proofs that the setting up of the Kingdom of God

---

6. *Watch Tower Reprints*, I, p. 817.

is already begun, that it is pointed out in prophecy as due to begin the exercise of power in A.D. 1878, and that the "battle of the great day of God Almighty" (Rev. 16:14.), which will end in A.D. 1914 with the complete overthrow of earth's present rulership, is already commenced. The gathering of the armies is plainly visible from the standpoint of God's Word.[7]

In the observations to open the year 1894 in *Zion's Watch Tower* the reader is informed that "worldly people not only see the great 'battle' approaching, but they see the skirmishing is already beginning all along the line. . . ."[8]

In the July 15, 1894, *Zion's Watch Tower*, under the heading "Can It Be Delayed until 1914?" C. T. Russell wrote:

> Seventeen years ago people said, concerning the time features presented in MILLENNIAL DAWN, They seem reasonable in many respects, but surely no such radical changes could occur between now and the close of 1914: if you had proved that they would come about in a century or two, it would seem much more probable.
>
> What changes have since occurred, and what velocity is gained daily? "The old is quickly passing and the new is coming in."
>
> Now, in view of recent labor troubles and threatened anarchy, our readers are writing to know if there may not be a mistake in the 1914 date. They say that they do not see how present conditions can hold out so long under the strain.
>
> We see no reason for changing the figures—nor could we change them if we would. They are, we believe, God's dates, not ours. But bear in mind that the end of 1914 is not the date for the *beginning*, but for the *end* of the time of trouble.[9]

---

7. P. 101. The 1915 edition of this text changed the "A.D. 1914" to read "A.D. 1915."

8. *Watch Tower Reprints*, II (January 1, 1894), p. 1605.

9. *Watch Tower Reprints*, II, p. 1677.

In 1904 Russell stressed the importance of 1910–1912:

According to our expectations the stress of the great time of trouble will be on us soon, somewhere between 1910 and 1912—culminating with the end of the "Times of the Gentiles," October, 1914.

The beginning of the severity of the trouble is not distinctly marked in the Scriptures, and is rather conjectural. We infer that so great a trouble, so world-wide a catastrophe, could scarcely be accomplished in less than three years, and that if it lasted much more than three years "no flesh would be saved."[10]

A number of statements Russell made in 1914, 1915, and 1916 in reference to Armageddon and the establishment of Messiah's Kingdom are significant.

*May 1, 1914.*

There is absolutely no ground for Bible students to question that the consummation of this Gospel age is now even at the door, and that it will end as the Scriptures foretell in a great time of trouble such as never was since there was a nation. We see the participants in this great crisis banding themselves together. . . . The great crisis, the great clash, symbolically represented as a fire, that will consume the ecclesiastical heavens and the social earth, is very near.[11]

*September 1, 1914.*

While it is possible that Armageddon may begin next Spring, yet it is purely speculation to attempt to say just when. We see, however, that there are parallels between the close of the Jewish age and this Gospel age. These

---

10. *The New Creation* (Brooklyn: Watch Tower Bible and Tract Society, 1904), p. 579.

11. *Watch Tower Reprints*, VI (May 1, 1914), p. 5450.

parallels seem to point to the year just before us—particularly the early months.[12]

*December 14, 1914.*

Few of the awakening ones realize that the present war is permitted for the weakening of the nations, preparatory to the utter collapse of the Present Order of things—and the ushering in of the New Order—the Reign of Righteousness, under Messiah's Kingdom.[13]

*April 1, 1915.*

The Battle of Armageddon, to which this war is leading, will be a great contest between right and wrong, and will signify the complete and everlasting overthrow of the wrong, and the permanent establishment of Messiah's righteous kingdom for the blessing of the world. . . . Our sympathies are broad enough to cover all engaged in the dreadful strife, as our hope is broad enough and deep enough to include all in the great blessings which our Master and his Millennial kingdom are about to bring to the world.[14]

*September 1, 1916.*

We see no reason for doubting, therefore, that the Times of the Gentiles ended in October, 1914; and that a few more years will witness their utter collapse and the full establishment of God's kingdom in the hands of Messiah.[15]

*Sometime during the War.*

The present great war in Europe is the beginning of the Armageddon of the Scriptures. (Rev. 16:16-20.) It will eventuate in the complete overthrow of all the systems of error which have so long oppressed the people of God and deluded the world. . . . We believe the present war cannot last much longer until revolution shall break out.[16]

---

12. *Watch Tower Reprints*, VI (September 1, 1914), p. 5527.
13. *New York Times*, December 14, 1914, p. 6.
14. *Watch Tower Reprints*, VI (April 1, 1915), p. 5659.
15. *Watch Tower Reprints*, VI (September 1, 1916), p. 5950.
16. C. T. Russell, *Pastor Russell's Sermons*, p. 676.

*The Finished Mystery* stated to be the "Posthumous Work of Pastor Russell" (p. 2) applies the events formerly scheduled to come in 1914 and before, to the period of 1918–1925. When some of the explanations given in the first edition did not transpire as predicted, a later edition (the edition used was dated 1926) altered the statements and dates. Quotations from this volume with changes noted are given without comment.

> . . . The Spring of 1918 will bring upon Christendom a spasm of anguish greater even than that experienced in the Fall of 1914. . . . The travail that is coming is to be upon nominal Zion—"Christendom," "Babylon"; and it will be a great and sore affliction—"A Time of Trouble such as was not since there was a nation." (p. 62)

As the fleshly-minded apostates from Christianity, siding with the radicals and revolutionaries, will rejoice at the inheritance of desolation that will be Christendom's after 1918, so will God do to the successful revolutionary movement; it shall be utterly desolated, "even all of it." Not one vestige of it shall survive the ravages of world-wide all-embracing anarchy, in the fall of 1920. (Rev. 11:7-13) [The 1926 ed. reads: "in the end of the time of trouble."] (p. 542)

Pastor Russell's mission, in large part, was to advise Christendom of its impending end, in the time of world-wide trouble. It is the Divine judgment upon the nations. . . . There will be no chance of escaping from destruction, through the nations. . . . The trouble is due to the dawning of the Day of Christ, the Millennium. It is the Day of Vengeance, which began in the world war of 1914 and which will break like a furious morning storm in 1918.— Lam. 4:18. (p. 404)

Some interesting developments in connection with the setting up of the Kingdom may occur in 1920, six years after the great Time of Trouble began. It would not be strange if this were so, when we recall that after forty years wandering in the wilderness the Israelites came into possession of the land of Canaan after a further six years. As these matters are still future we can but wait to see. We anticipate that the "earthquake" will occur early in 1918, and that the "fire" will come in the fall of 1920. [Comments on Revelation 11:13. The 1926 ed. reads: "and that the 'fire' will follow in due course."] (p. 178)

This vision of the prophet Ezekiel depicts the established theocratic Kingdom of God on earth, civil and religious, spiritual and earthly. . . . The Temple . . . is a type and symbol of "better things to come," after the wars, revolutions and anarchy of the period from 1914 to 1925 have passed. [The 1926 ed. reads: "of the time of trouble have passed."] (p. 569)[17]

On February 24, 1918, Judge Rutherford "delivered for the first time the lecture that later became entitled 'Millions Now Living Will Never Die.' " This was followed by a "Millions Now Living Will Never Die" campaign from 1918 to 1921 and a book by the same title.[18] The stage was being set for the new emphasis on 1925.

### 1920–1929

Published late in 1920, Rutherford's *Millions Now Living Will Never Die* booklet and the campaign which promoted it created quite a stir. The essence of this new stress was that the Kingdom would be set up in 1925.

Based upon the argument heretofore set forth, then, that the old order of things, the old world, is ending and is therefore passing away, and that the new order is coming in, and that 1925 shall mark the resurrection of the faithful worthies of old and the beginning of reconstruction, it is reasonable to conclude that millions of people now on the earth will be still on the earth in 1925. Then, based

17. Clayton J. Woodworth and George H. Fisher (eds.), (Brooklyn: People's Pulpit Association, 1917).
18. *Jehovah's Witnesses in the Divine Purpose*, pp. 76, 140.

upon the promises set forth in the divine Word, we must reach the positive and indisputable conclusion that millions now living will never die.[19]

After the quotation and explanation of Isaiah 35:10, Rutherford looked to the immediate future:

This is the Golden Age of which the prophets prophesied and of which the Psalmist sang; and it is the privilege of the student of the divine Word today, by the eye of faith, to see that we are standing at the very portals of that blessed time! Let us look up and lift up our heads. Deliverance is at the door![20]

The booklet and the campaign made many new converts, but as 1925 approached Rutherford became less sure of his predictions, and by early 1925 he had acknowledged the failure of his expectations.[21]

In 1929, with the publication of *Life*, attention was switched from the 1925 failure to a new issue. The premise of this new book was that the time of the end was very close because the Jews were returning to Palestine.

If the end of 1925 marks the end of the last fifty-year period, then it follows that we should expect the people to begin to receive some knowledge concerning God's great plan of restoration. The Jews are to have the favors first, and thereafter all others who obey the Lord.[22]

That the return of the Jews to God's favor means the time when God will extend the privileges of life to the people, both the dead and the living, is shown by the words written [quotes Romans 11:15, 16]. . . .[23]

19. Brooklyn: International Bible Students Association (1920), p. 97.
20. *Ibid.*, p. 105.
21. Timothy White, *A People for His Name* (New York: Vantage Press, 1967), p. 194.
22. Brooklyn: Watch Tower Bible and Tract Society, p. 170.
23. *Ibid.*, p. 332.

That foreshadowed God's purpose now to shortly dash to pieces the Devil's organization that controls all the nations of the earth, and then bring peace and prosperity to the people; and all who obey him will be granted life everlasting on the earth.[24]

The thesis of *Life* was discarded only about a year after its publication.[25]

The year 1929 witnessed two other testimonies to the soon end of the world. One was the publication of the book *Prophecy*, the other was the building of "Beth Sarim" ("House of the Princes") in San Diego. In *Prophecy* Rutherford stated: "Satan knows that shortly he must fight the Lord, and therefore he prepares for the conflict."[26] In concluding the chapter on Armageddon the shortness of the time was again stressed:

By the proclaiming of the doings of Jehovah and his purposes the people may now know the meaning of the present-day events, and what shall shortly come to pass, and what will be for their good.[27]

"Beth Sarim" was built to provide a place to which the "princes," Abraham, Isaac, Jacob, and others might return just before the closing events of the end. The *San Diego Sun* of March 15, 1930, reported,

The seven famous men will not have long to rest at their San Diego estate because they soon will lead the forces of the Lord to vanquish the minions of Satan at the Battle of Armageddon, Rutherford believes.

"Beth Sarim" was sold by the Society shortly after Rutherford's death in 1942.

---

24. *Ibid.*, pp. 346, 347.
25. W. J. Schnell, *Thirty Years a Watch Tower Slave* (Grand Rapids: Baker Book House, 1956), pp. 90, 91.
26. Brooklyn: Watch Tower Bible and Tract Society (1929), p. 266.
27. *Ibid.*, p. 298.

## 1930–1939

The decade 1930–1939 saw the abandoning of specific date setting, but readers of the Watchtower material were assured that the Battle of Armageddon was near. Rutherford explained the new position for this period:

> There was a measure of disappointment on the part of Jehovah's faithful ones on earth concerning the years 1914, 1918 and 1925, which disappointment lasted for a time. Later the faithful learned that these dates were definitely fixed in the Scriptures; and they also learned to quit fixing dates for the future and predicting what would come to pass on a certain date, but to rely (and they do rely) upon the Word of God as to the events that must come to pass.[28]

In *Light*, Volume II, Rutherford wrote, "The great climax is at hand. The kings of earth now set themselves against his anointed Stone."[29] A year later, the first of three volumes of *Vindication* appeared, in which Rutherford warned:

> God's kingdom has begun to operate. His day of vengeance is here, and Armageddon is at hand and certain to fall upon Christendom, and that within an early date. God's judgment is upon Christendom and must shortly be executed.[30]

In his study on the Jehovah's Witnesses, Herbert H. Stroup commented on the continuing importance of the theme of the booklet *Millions Now Living Will Never Die*, even in the early 1930's:

> The theme of the booklet was so rich an energizer of his followers and so compelling an idea in itself that even as late as 1932 Mr. Rutherford was still delivering talks upon

28. *Vindication* (Brooklyn: Watch Tower Bible and Tract Society, 1931), I, pp. 338, 339.
29. Brooklyn: Watch Tower Bible and Tract Society (1930), II, p. 327.
30. I, p. 147.

it. In that year he declared that the religious work of the Witnesses was "coming to a conclusion," that the end was "only a short time away," and that the end was "much less than the length of a generation."[31]

The book *Salvation* (1939) also stressed the nearness of Armageddon:

The abundance of Scriptural evidence, together with the physical facts that have come to pass showing the fulfillment of prophecy, conclusively proves that the time for the battle of the great day of God Almighty is very near and that in that battle all of God's enemies shall be destroyed and the earth cleared of wickedness. . . .[32]

Likewise today, all the nations and peoples of earth are face to face with the greatest emergency. They are being warned as God commands, that the disaster of Armageddon is just ahead.[33]

### 1940–1949

Rutherford's book *Religion* concluded with the chapter "End of Religion," in which he wrote:

The prophecies of Almighty God, the fulfillment of which now clearly appears from the physical facts, show that the end of religion has come and with its end the complete downfall of Satan's entire organization.[34]

. . . The day for final settlement is near at hand.[35]

The year 1940 seemed to be very close to the termination of this "system of things," for Rutherford wrote the following in *The Watchtower*:

31. *The Jehovah's Witnesses* (New York: Columbia University Press, 1945), p. 55.
32. J. F. Rutherford (Brooklyn: Watchtower Bible and Tract Society, 1939), p. 310.
33. *Ibid.*, p. 361.
34. Brooklyn: Watchtower Bible and Tract Society (1940), p. 336.
35. *Ibid.*, p. 338.

The witness work for THE THEOCRACY appears to be about done in most of the countries of "Christendom." . . .

. . . Now the totalitarian rule has suppressed the Theocratic message, and it should be expected that when they quit fighting amongst themselves all the totalitarian rulers will turn their attention to the complete suppression of everything pertaining to the THEOCRATIC GOVERNMENT.

What, then, does it mean that the THEOCRATIC GOVERNMENT is now suppressed in many nations? It means that the hour is rapidly approaching when the "sign" of Armageddon will be clearly revealed and all who are on the side of Jehovah will see and appreciate it.[36]

Herbert Stroup reported the following incident which occurred shortly before Christmas in 1940. "The wife declared that she would never again celebrate Christmas, but added with a shrug of her shoulders, 'I should worry. The kingdom may be here before Christmas.' "[37]

In Rutherford's book *Children*, the touching story of two young Jehovah's Witnesses is told. John, twenty, and Eunice, eighteen, who are deeply in love, decided that their marriage should be postponed until after Armageddon and the impending establishment of the Kingdom. John is made to say:

Armageddon is surely near, and during that time the Lord will clean off the earth everything that offends and is disagreeable. . . . From now on we shall have our heart devotion fixed on THE THEOCRACY, knowing that soon we shall journey forever together in the earth. Our hope is that within a few years our marriage may be consummated and, by the Lord's grace, we shall have sweet children that

36. *The Watchtower*, September 1, 1940, p. 265. White (p. 335) quotes from the *1942 Yearbook* (p. 29), completed by Rutherford just before his death: "The record as herewith published would, on the face of it, show that the Theocratic witness work on earth is about done."
37. P. 142.

will be an honor to the Lord. We can well defer our marriage until lasting peace comes to the earth.[38]

The publication of *The New World*, the first book after Rutherford's death, continued to carry the theme of the closeness of the end and the soon-to-be-realized new world:

> . . . THE NEW WORLD IS AT THE DOORS. . . . The time is short. Those who do not inform themselves and who do not now choose the new world which Higher Powers shall establish will never live to enter into blessings and glories.[39]

In 1943 the book *The Truth Shall Make You Free* warned:

> The final war will come as a most sudden and complete surprise. . . . Nevertheless, the appearing of the "desolating abomination in the holy place" is an unerring proof that the unknown day and hour of the beginning of the final war is dangerously near.[40]

It was in the same book that the first revised chronology since Russell's was published. Russell's chronology made the 6,000 years since Adam's creation run out in 1872. The new chronology had the same period run out in 1972. The chapter titled "The Count of Time" concluded: "We are therefore near the end of six thousand years of human history, with conditions upon us and tremendous events at hand foreshadowed by those of Noah's day.—Luke 17:26-30."[41]

That this new chronology did establish in the minds of many Witnesses a new date for when Armageddon might take place is illustrated by the experience of Marcus Bach with the Witnesses, as reported in 1946. Bach asked a Witness why he sacrificed as he did; the reply and the conversation are given:

---

38. Brooklyn: Watchtower Bible and Tract Society (1941), p. 366.
39. Brooklyn: Watchtower Bible and Tract Society (1942), p. 10.
40. P. 341.
41. *Ibid.*, p. 152.

150

"Armageddon." "Scheduled for when?" "It should come sometime before 1972." He made it sound so commonplace we might have been talking about the weather. And yet, for him, Armageddon would be life's most portentous event.[42]

Bach also records an interesting conversation on children and marriage:

"Do you have any children?" His answer was sincere but impersonal. "No, we haven't. We think it is better to wait until after Armageddon." . . . "Is this a belief among the Witnesses," I asked, "or is it just your idea?" "The Society feels that since the time of the end is so near, people can witness more effectively if they do not have too many responsibilities."[43]

In 1944 the establishment of an "international peace organization" was seen

as one of the most positive evidences that "the kingdom of heaven is at hand" and that the end of the world arrangement is now near, Jesus foretold the setting up of that antichrist organization.[44]

In 1946 it was stated that "the disaster of Armageddon, greater than that which befell Sodom and Gomorrah, is at the door."[45]

## 1950–Present

It is not necessary to quote extensively from the writings of

42. *They Have Found a Faith* (New York: Bobbs-Merrill Company, 1946), p. 34.

43. *Ibid.*, p. 44. See the same emphasis in the August 7, 1969, issue of *New Society*, p. 201: "Were they planning to have a family out in South America, then? 'No,' said Liz. 'We've decided not to have any children till after Armageddon.'"

44. *The Kingdom Is at Hand* (Brooklyn: Watchtower Bible and Tract Society, 1944), p. 342.

45. *Let God Be True* (Brooklyn: Watchtower Bible and Tract Society, 1946), p. 194.

the period between 1950 and 1974 to establish that they too stress the nearness of Armageddon. Several examples of statements should suffice.

In *This Means Everlasting Life* urgency is stressed:

> Every intelligent creature on earth must determine his own destiny. Now at the consummation of this system of things when the judgment of the nations is under way and the separating of the sheep and the goats with opposite destinies is nearing a conclusion, yes, now is the urgent time to make your determination.[46]

> The march is on! Where? To the field of Armageddon for the "war of the great day of God the Almighty"! God will not hear the unscriptural prayers of all the religious clergy combined on "world prayer" days for the sparing of this old world from Armageddon. It is unavoidable, for Jehovah's time has come to settle definitely the issue of universal sovereignty.[47]

According to the observations of ex-Witness Stan Thomas, and other authors as well, the 1953 convention of the Jehovah's Witnesses in Yankee Stadium was of special significance:

> . . . the Witnesses were warned to expect an all out attack by Satan's forces (the world) in the near future, an event which would be the spark to ignite Armageddon. As to precisely when this attack was to be expected the Watchtower Society has grown much too wise to officially speculate, but many Witnesses, particularly older ones, felt that 1954 could well be "The Year." After all, Russell's "preparatory work" took exactly forty years and ended in 1914. Was it not likely that a further period of forty years, commencing in 1914, would see "the end of all things"?[48]

In 1955 the Witnesses were told that "in the light of the

---

46. Brooklyn: Watchtower Bible and Tract Society (1950), p. 307.
47. *Ibid.*, p. 311.
48. *Jehovah's Witnesses and What They Believe* (Grand Rapids: Zondervan Publishing House, 1967), pp. 54, 55.

fulfillment of Bible prophecy it is becoming clear that the war of Armageddon is nearing its breaking-out point."[49]

It was stated in 1963 that "it does no good to use Bible chronology for speculating on dates that are still future in the stream of time.—Matt. 24:36."[50] Yet the year 1966 saw just such speculation on the basis of viewing the 6,000 year chronology as running out in 1975.[51]

Without intending to, the Jehovah's Witnesses have, in addition to the evidence presented, identified themselves as guilty of "false prophesying"—of being false prophets. The October 8, 1968, issue of *Awake!* makes the following statement:

> True, there have been those in times past who predicted an *"end to the world,"* even announcing a specific date. . . . Yet, nothing happened. The "end" did not come. *They were guilty of false prophesying.* Why? What was missing?
>
> Missing was the full measure of evidence required in fulfillment of Bible prophecy. *Missing from such people were God's truths and the evidence that he was guiding and using them* [italics added].[52]

Obviously such a statement must refer to the Watchtower Society and *The Watchtower* itself as the February 1, 1938, issue demonstrates:

> *As far back as 1880* The Watchtower *pointed to A.D. 1914 as the date marking the end of the world,* at which time great trouble would come upon the nations; but at that

49. *You May Survive Armageddon into God's New World* (Brooklyn: Watchtower Bible and Tract Society, 1955), p. 331.

50. *All Scripture Is Inspired by God and Beneficial* (Brooklyn: Watchtower Bible and Tract Society, 1963), p. 286. See also the contrast between how Matthew 24:36 is viewed here and in *The Watchtower* issue of August 15, 1968, pp. 500, 501.

51. This section, which begins with the quote from the 1886 issue of *Zion's Watch Tower*, is taken from my book *The Jehovah's Witnesses and Prophetic Speculation*, pp. 83-93.

52. P. 23.

time it was not seen by God's people on earth that the trouble would be the battle of Jehovah against Satan's organization. For many years it was believed by them, and so stated in *The Watchtower*, that "the time of trouble" would be a terrific clash between the various elements of the earth, such as capital and labor. Not until 1925 was "the time of trouble" Scripturally understood . . . [italics added].[53]

If anything has been proved by the materials of the Watchtower Society, it is that this "prophet" is certainly a false one, because its words have fallen "to the earth" (I Sam. 3:19 NWT). And as the *Awake!* writer said of those "guilty of false prophesying": "Missing from such people were God's truths and the evidence that he was guiding and using them."

### The Watchtower "Prophet" Further Tested

The third test for the identification of a true prophet of God cited by the Jehovah's Witnesses (Deut. 13:1-4) is that "his prophesyings must promote true worship, being in harmony with God's revealed word and commandments."[54] The testimonies of many former Jehovah's Witnesses indicate that they did not find true worship in this organization because Jesus Christ was not given His proper place. As Jehovah's Witnesses they could not say with Thomas as he addressed Jesus: "My Lord and my God" (John 20:28). They could not in its fullest meaning "worship" Jesus Christ (Matt. 8:2; 9:18; 14:33; 15:25; 28:9, 17; John 9:35-38; Heb. 1:6).

Many books have been written which show that the Witnesses' teachings are not in full "harmony with God's revealed word and commandments." The Witnesses debate this and claim that their explanations of biblical truth emanate from Jehovah God. They state that to their organization "alone

---

53. P. 35, para. 3.
54. *Aid to Bible Understanding*, p. 1348.

154

Bethel Home (left), headquarters of the Watchtower Bible and Tract Society, Brooklyn

God's Sacred Word, the Bible, is not a sealed book."[55] It has already been seen that such a claim is not in agreement with the evidence.

Further proof that the Watchtower Society has brought contradiction and chaos to the understanding of the Bible is illustrated in my tract "Is the Watchtower Society God's Channel?" which is reproduced here.

---

55. *The Watchtower*, July 1, 1973, p. 402.

# IS THE WATCHTOWER SOCIETY
# GOD'S CHANNEL?

The Watchtower Bible and Tract Society, the governing body of Jehovah's Witnesses, identifies itself as God's "sole collective channel for the flow of Biblical truth to men on earth" in these last days (*The Watchtower*, July 15, 1960, p. 439). How long has God used the Society?

"The WATCH TOWER BIBLE AND TRACT SOCIETY is the greatest corporation in the world, because from the time of its organization until now the Lord has used it as His channel through which to make known the Glad Tidings" (*The Watch Tower*, 1917, p. 22, quoted in *Studies in the Scriptures*, VII, p. 144).

It is claimed that Bible translations and interpretations emanate from God. " They are passed to the Holy Spirit who invisibly communicates with Jehovah's Witnesses— and the publicity department" according to F. W. Franz, Vice-President of the Watchtower Society (*Scottish Daily Express*, Nov. 24, 1954). In the treatment which follows, ten examples — hundreds could be given — show that the lofty Watchtower claims find no support in an examination of Watchtower publications.

1. Ruth—from historical book to book of prophecy.

STATEMENT: "While the book of Ruth is not prophetical, but merely historical, it is valuable to us in various ways" (*Watch Tower Reprints,* IV, Nov. 15, 1902, p. 3110).

CONTRADICTION: "Not only is the book historical, but it is prophetic, the fulfilment of which prophecy takes place in these present days . . . . We must conclude that the book of Ruth was made part of God's Word or message as a prophecy for the special benefit of the remnant in the last days. . . . the book is a prophecy" (J. F. Rutherford, *Preservation*, pp. 169, 175, 176).

2. Abaddon, Apollyon—from Satan to Jesus Christ. This example relates to Revelation 9:11 and the identification of the angel of the bottomless pit.

STATEMENT: " 'The prince of the power of the air.' Eph. 2:2 . . . That is, Destroyer. But in plain English his name is Satan, the Devil" (*Studies in the Scriptures*, VII, p. 159).

CONTRADICTION: "In Hebrew his name is Abaddon, meaning 'Destruction'; and in the Greek it is Apollyon, meaning 'Destroyer.' All this plainly identifies the 'angel' as picturing Jesus Christ, the Son of Jehovah God" (*Then is Finished the Mystery of God*, p. 232).

3. Adam—from resurrection to no resurrection.

STATEMENT: "Just when Adam will be awakened, only the Lord knows. It may be early or it may be late during the period of restoration" (J. F. Rutherford, *Reconciliation*, pp. 323, 324).

CONTRADICTIONS: "There is no promise found in the Scriptures that Adam's redemption and resurrection and salvation will take place at any time. Adam had a fair trial for life and completely failed" (J. F. Rutherford, *Salvation*, p. 43). In recent writings, Adam and Eve are viewed as among those who are incorrigible sinners who "proved that they were not worthy of life, and they will not be resurrected" (*From Paradise Lost to Paradise Regained*, p. 236).

4. Sodom and Gomorrah—resurrection promised, resurrection denied, resurrection reinstated.

STATEMENT: "Thus our Lord teaches that the Sodomites did not have a full opportunity; and he guarantees them such opportunity . . ." (C. T. Russell, *Studies in the Scriptures*, I, p. 110).

CONTRADICTION: "He was pinpointing the utter impossibility of ransom for unbelievers or those willfully wicked, because Sodom and Gomorrah were irrevocably condemned and destroyed, beyond any possible recovery" (*The Watchtower*, February 1, 1954, p. 85).

RETURN TO FORMER POSITION: "As in the case of Tyre and Sidon, Jesus showed that Sodom, bad as it was, had not got to the state of being unable to repent . . . So the spiritual recovery of the dead people of Sodom is not hopeless" (*The Watchtower*, March 1, 1965, p. 139).

5. Worship of Jesus Christ—from acceptance to rejection.

STATEMENTS: "*Question* . . . . Was he *really* worshiped, or is the translation faulty? *Answer*. Yes, we believe our Lord while on earth was really worshiped, and properly so . . . . It was proper for our Lord to receive worship . . ." (*Watch Tower Reprints*, III, July 15, 1898, p. 2337). "He was the object of unreproved worship even when a babe, by the wise men who came to see the new-born king . . . . He never reproved any for acts of worship offered to Himself . . . . Had Christ not been *more* than man the same reason would have prevented Him from receiving worship . . . " (*Watch Tower Reprints*, I, Oct., 1880, p. 144)."The purposes of this Society are: . . . public Christian worship of Almighty God and Jesus Christ; to arrange for and hold local and world-wide assemblies for such worship . . ." (*Charter of the Watch Tower Society of Pennsylvania*, Article II).

CONTRADICTIONS: ". . . No distinct worship is to be rendered to Jesus Christ now glorified in heaven. Our worship is to go to Jehovah God" (*The Watchtower*, Jan. 1, 1954, p. 31). "For example, the magi from the east and King Herod said they wanted to 'do obeisance to' (*proskyneo*) the babe that had been born king of the Jews. 'Do obeisance' is preferable here because neither the magi nor King Herod meant to worship the babe as God" (*The Watchtower*, May 15, 1954, p. 317).

Hebrews 1:6 is a special problem for the Jehovah's Witnesses because it clearly states that the angels are commanded to *worship* Christ: ". . . And let all the angels of God worship him." In an attempt to explain away the meaning of worship a Witness writer concluded: "If the rendering 'worship' is preferred, then it must be understood that such 'worship' is only of a relative kind" (*The Watchtower*, Nov. 15, 1970, p. 704). Yet such an explanation is rejected in *Make Sure of All Things*, p. 178! "Bowing before men or angels as 'relative' w o r s h i p forbidden." (Good discussions on the subject of worship given to Christ are to be found in Anthony A. Hoekema's *The Four Major Cults*, pp. 339-344 and F. W. Thomas' *Masters of Deception*, pp. 29-37).

6. Resurrection from the dead—from all to some.

STATEMENTS: "All are to be awakened from the Adamic death, as though from a sleep, by virtue of the ransom given . . . " (C. T. Russell, *Studies in the Scriptures*, V, p. 478). "Under this new covenant the whole human race shall have the opportunity to come back to God through Christ the mediator" (J. F. Rutherford, *The Harp of God*, p. 328 or 334, according to edition).

CONTRADICTION: "It has been held by many that the Scriptures guarantee that 'all must come back from the dead' at Christ's return and during his thousand-year rule. (*Studies in the Scriptures*, Volume Five, pages 478-486). That conclusion does not appear to have support in reason or in the Scriptures" (J. F. Rutherford, *Salvation*, p. 224).

7. Israel—literal Israel to spiritual Israel.

STATEMENTS: "That the re-establishment of Israel in the land of Palestine is one of the events to be expected in this Day of the Lord, we are fully assured by the above expression of the Prophet [commenting on Amos 9:11, 14, 15]. Notice, particularly, that the prophecy cannot be interpreted in any symbolic sense" (C. T. Russell, *Studies in the Scriptures*, III, p. 244). "The promise, time and again repeated, that the Lord would regather them and bless them in the land and *keep them there* and bless them for ever is conclusive proof that the promise must be fulfilled . . . . Behold, that time is now at hand!" (J. F. Rutherford, *Comfort for the Jews*, p. 55). (See also Rutherford's *Life*.)

CONTRADICTION: "Nothing in the modern return of Jews to Palestine and the setting up of the Israeli republic corresponds with the Bible

prophecies concerning the restoration of Jehovah's name-people to his favor and organization. . . . The remnant of spiritual Israelites, as Jehovah's Witnesses, have proclaimed world-wide the establishment of God's kingdom in 1914" (*Let God Be True*, second ed., pp. 217, 218).

8. "And the name of the star is called Wormwood" (Rev. 8:11)— three differing interpretations.

STATEMENT: "Calvin is entitled to the honor of having at one time been a papal star . . . . *Is called Wormwood*. —What an ideal name for the doctrine which has caused more bitterness against God than any other doctrine ever taught, and for the man who roasted Servetus at the stake" (*Studies in the Scriptures*, VII, p. 151).

CONTRADICTION: "The 'great star' falling from heaven as a burning lamp was Satan . . . . The name of this star is called 'Wormwood', which means bitter. Being cast out of heaven Satan is in the 'gall of bitterness' " (J. F. Rutherford, *Light*, I, pp. 126, 127).

CONTRADICTION: "In view of these features about it, what religious class of people could this blazing, falling 'great star' picture but the apostate Christian clergy of Christendom, Catholic, Orthodox and Protestant and otherwise sectarian? . . . But what should have been spiritual 'water' to sustain the spiritual life of the peoples, the apostate Christian clergy have turned into undrinkable, deadly, bitter wormwood waters . . . false, pagan, unchristian, unbiblical doctrines . . . (*Then is Finished the Mystery of God*, pp. 224, 225).

9. The "superior authorities" of Romans 13.

STATEMENT: Until 1929 it was taught that the "higher powers" or "superior authorities" *(New World Translation)* were the earthly rulers to whom the Christian paid taxes, etc. (C. T. Russell, *Studies in the Scriptures,* I, p. 266).

CONTRADICTION: From 1929 to 1962 the "superior authorities" were explained as "the Most High God Jehovah and his exalted Son Jesus Christ" *(This Means Everlasting Life,* p. 197).

RETURN TO FORMER POSITION: "In spite of the end of the Gentile Times in 1914, God permitted the political authorities of this world to continue as the 'higher powers' or the 'powers that be,' which are 'ordained of God'" *(Babylon the Great Has Fallen! God's Kingdom Rules!,* p. 548).

10. The Great Multitude as a spiritual class—yes, no.

STATEMENTS: *"Does the Great Company receive life direct from God on the spirit plane? Answer—* Yes, they receive life direct in that they have been begotten of the Holy Spirit, and when they are begotten they are just the same way as the little flock, because we are called in the one hope of our calling. They do not make their calling and election sure, but not being worthy of second death, they therefore receive life on the spirit plane" *(What Pastor Russell Said,* p. 297). "Ever and anon someone advances the conclusion that the 'great multitude' will not be a spiritual class. The prophecy of Ezekiel shows that such conclusion is erroneous. The fact that their position is seven steps higher than the outside shows that they must be made spirit creatures . . . They must be spirit creatures in order to be in the outer court of the divine structure, described by Ezekiel" (J. F. Rutherford, *Vindication,* III, p. 204).

CONTRADICTION: "Thus the great multitude is definitely identified, not as a spirit-begotten class whose hopes are for a place in heaven, but a class trusting in the Lord, and who hope for everlasting life on earth . . ." (J. F. Rutherford, *Riches,* pp. 324, 325).

## CONCLUSION

Do these examples support the claim that the Watchtower Bible and Tract Society "from the time of its organization until now" has been God's "sole collective channel for the flow of Biblical truth to men on earth?" Do they support the claim that Witness interpretations emanate from God? Let the reader read and apply the following statements found in Watchtower material.

"Jehovah never makes any mistakes. Where the student relies upon man, he is certain to be led into difficulties" (J. F. Rutherford, *Prophecy,* pp. 67, 68).

"Men not only contradict God, they contradict one another. How can they be reliable guides—unless their words are based on God's words? But how can you know whether they are or not? By going directly to God's Word as your source of authority. Search for yourself and let God be true!" *(Awake! March 22, 1963,* p. 32).

Many former Jehovah's Witnesses can testify to having come free of this organization because of "going directly to God's Word" as their source of authority and enlightenment.

159

**Figure 5**

sponding parallel in that typical dispensation, so we find that this most noteworthy event taught by the jubilee has its corresponding parallel. Our Lord's presence as Bridegroom, Reaper and King is shown in both dispensations. Even the movement on the part of the virgins going forth to meet him, their disappointment and the tarrying time of thirty years find their parallel both in time and circumstances. And the parallelism continues to the full end of the harvest of this dispensation—until the overthrow of the professedly Christian kingdoms, really "kingdoms of this world," and the full establishment of the Kingdom of God in the earth at A. D. 1914, the terminus of the Times of the Gentiles. (See Vol. II., chap. iv.) This coming trouble and overthrow, we have seen, had its parallel in the destruction of Jerusalem and the complete overthrow of the Jewish polity, A. D. 70—another parallel, corresponding in both time and circumstances.

Again, we have found the second advent of our Lord indicated by the prophet Daniel (12:1), yet in such a manner as to be under cover until the events foretold to precede it had transpired and passed into history, when we were led to see that the one vailed under the name Michael is indeed that which the name indicates—*God's representative*—"The Great Prince." Yes, we recognize him: "The Prince of the Covenant," the "Mighty God [ruler]," the "Everlasting Father [life-giver]" (Dan. 11:22; Isa. 9:6), who is to "stand up" with power and authority, to accomplish the great restitution of all things, and to offer everlasting life to the dead and dying millions of mankind, redeemed by his own precious blood. And, having traced the 1335 days of Dan. xii., down to their ending at this same date, we can now understand why the angel who thus pointed out the date referred to it in such exultant terms—"Oh, the blessedness of him that waiteth [who is in a wait-

sponding parallel in that typical dispensation, so we find that this most noteworthy event taught by the jubilee has its corresponding parallel. Our Lord's presence as Bridegroom, Reaper and King is shown in both dispensations. Even the movement on the part of the virgins going forth to meet him, their disappointment and the tarrying time of thirty years find their parallel both in time and circumstances. And the parallelism continues to the full end of the harvest of this dispensation—until the overthrow of the professedly Christian kingdoms, really "kingdoms of this world," and the full establishment of the Kingdom of God in the earth after 1914, the terminus of the Times of the Gentiles. (See Vol. II., chap. iv.) This coming trouble and overthrow, we have seen, had its parallel in the destruction of Jerusalem and the complete overthrow of the Jewish polity, A. D. 70—another parallel, corresponding in both time and circumstances.

Again, we have found the second advent of our Lord indicated by the prophet Daniel (12:1), yet in such a manner as to be under cover until the events foretold to precede it had transpired and passed into history, when we were led to see that the one vailed under the name Michael is indeed that which the name indicates—*God's representative*—"The Great Prince." Yes, we recognize him: "The Prince of the Covenant," the "Mighty God [ruler]," the "Everlasting Father [life-giver]" (Dan. 11:22; Isa. 9:6), who is to "stand up" with power and authority, to accomplish the great restitution of all things, and to offer everlasting life to the dead and dying millions of mankind, redeemed by his own precious blood. And, having traced the 1335 days of Dan. xii., down to their ending at this same date, we can now understand why the angel who thus pointed out the date referred to it in such exultant terms—"Oh, the blessedness of him that waiteth [who is in a wait-

An important change in Russell's *Thy Kingdom Come* (1907 edition and 1925 edition were used) to salvage the 1914 failure.

# Figure 6

end. The measuring of this period and determining when the pit of trouble shall be reached are easy enough if we have a definite date—a point in the Pyramid from which to start. We have this date-mark in the junction of the "First Ascending Passage" with the "Grand Gallery." That point marks the birth of our Lord Jesus, as the "Well," 33 inches farther on, indicates his death. So, then, if we measure backward down the "First Ascending Passage" to its junction with the "Entrance Passage," we shall have a fixed date to mark upon the downward passage. This measure is 1542 inches, and indicates the year B. C. 1542, as the date at that point. Then measuring *down* the "Entrance Passage" from that point, to find the distance to the entrance of the "Pit," representing the great trouble and destruction with which this age is to close, when evil will be overthrown from power, we find it to be 3416 inches, symbolizing 3416 years from the above date, B. C. 1542. This calculation shows A. D. 1874 as marking the beginning of the period of trouble; for 1542 years B. C. plus 1874 years A. D. equals 3416 years. Thus the Pyramid witnesses that the close of 1874 was the *dreadanical beginning of the time of trouble* such as was not since there was a nation—no, nor ever shall be afterward. And thus it will be noted that this "Witness" fully corroborates the Bible testimony on this subject, as shown by the "Parallel Dispensations" in MILLENNIAL DAWN, VOL. II., Chap. vii.

Nor should any doubt the fact that the forty years of judgment and trouble began in the fall of 1874 because the trouble has not yet reached an unendurable stage; and because, in some respects, the period since that date has been one of great advancement in knowledge. Remember that all this is shown in the Great Pyramid and illustrated in the diagram of the "Pit" which was draughted by Prof. Smyth without any reference to its application.

end. The measuring of this period and determining when the pit of trouble shall be reached are easy enough if we have a definite date—a point in the Pyramid from which to start. We have this date-mark in the junction of the "First Ascending Passage" with the "Grand Gallery." That point marks the birth of our Lord Jesus, as the "Well," 33 inches farther on, indicates his death. So, then, if we measure backward down the "First Ascending Passage" to its junction with the "Entrance Passage," we shall have a fixed date to mark upon the downward passage. This measure is 1542 inches, and indicates the year B. C. 1542, as the date at that point. Then measuring *down* the "Entrance Passage" from that point, to find the distance to the entrance of the "Pit," representing the great trouble and destruction with which this age is to close, when evil will be overthrown from power, we find it to be 3457 inches, symbolizing 3457 years from the above date, B. C. 1542. This calculation shows A. D. 1915 as marking the beginning of the period of trouble; for 1542 years B. C. plus 1915 years A. D. equals 3457 years. Thus the Pyramid witnesses that the close of 1914 will be the beginning of the time of trouble such as was not since there was a nation—no, nor ever shall be afterward. And thus it will be noted that this "Witness" fully corroborates the Bible testimony on this subject, as shown by the "Parallel Dispensations" in MILLENNIAL DAWN, VOL. II., Chap. vii.

Nor should any doubt the fact that the forty years of "harvest" which began in the fall of 1874 because the trouble has not yet reached so portentous and unendurable a stage; and because, in some respects, the "harvest" period since that date has been one of great advancement in knowledge. Remember, too, that the Great Pyramid figures and illustrations including the diagram of the "Pit" were drafted by Prof. Smyth without any reference to this application.

Besides, we should remember that the Word of the Lord clearly shows that the judgments of this time of trouble will begin with the nominal Church, prepara-

A comparison of the early and late editions (those used were dated 1901 and 1907) of Russell's *Thy Kingdom Come* shows that the Great Pyramid was used to prove that 1874 began the greatest time of trouble the world had ever seen, and then it was "stretched" to prove that this same time of trouble would begin in 1914.

**Figure 7**

will be overthrown and dissolved; but we are living in a special and peculiar time, the "Day of Jehovah," in which matters culminate quickly; and it is written, "A short work will the Lord make upon the earth." (See Vol. I., chap. xv.) For the past eleven years these things have been preached and published substantially as set forth above; and in that brief time the development of influences and agencies for the undermining and overthrow of the strongest empires of earth has been wonderful. In that time Communism, Socialism and Nihilism sprang into vigorous existence, and already are causing great uneasiness among the rulers and high ones of earth, whose hearts are failing them for fear, and for looking after those things which are coming on the earth; for the present powers are being mightily shaken, and ultimately shall pass away with a great tumult.

In view of this strong Bible evidence concerning the Times of the Gentiles, we consider it an established truth that the final end of the kingdoms of this world, and the full establishment of the Kingdom of God, will be accomplished by the end of A. D. 1914. Then the prayer of the Church, ever since her Lord took his departure—"Thy Kingdom come"—will be answered; and under that wise and just administration, the whole earth will be filled with the glory of the Lord—with knowledge, and righteousness, and peace (Psa. 72:19; Isa. 6:3; Hab. 2:14); and the will of God shall be done "*on earth, as it is done in heaven.*"

Daniel's statement, that God's Kingdom will be set up, not after these kingdoms of earth are dissolved, but in their days, while they still exist and have power, and that it is God's Kingdom which shall break in pieces and consume all these kingdoms (Dan. 2:44), is worthy of our special consideration. So it was with each of these beastly governments: it existed before it acquired universal dominion. Babylon existed long before it conquered Jerusalem and

will be overthrown and dissolved; but we are living in a special and peculiar time, the "Day of Jehovah," in which matters culminate quickly; and it is written, "A short work will the Lord make upon the earth." (See Vol. I., chap. xv.) For the past eleven years these things have been preached and published substantially as set forth above; and in that brief time the development of influences and agencies for the undermining and overthrow of the strongest empires of earth has been wonderful. In that time Communism, Socialism and Nihilism sprang into vigorous existence, and already are causing great uneasiness among the rulers and high ones of earth, whose hearts are failing them for fear, and for looking after those things which are coming on the earth; for the present powers are being mightily shaken, and ultimately shall pass away with a great tumult.

In view of this strong Bible evidence concerning the Times of the Gentiles, we consider it an established truth that the final end of the kingdoms of this world, and the full establishment of the Kingdom of God, will be accomplished near the end of A.D. 1915. Then the prayer of the Church, ever since her Lord took his departure—"Thy Kingdom come"—will be answered; and under that wise and just administration, the whole earth will be filled with the glory of the Lord—with knowledge, and righteousness, and peace (Psa. 72:19; Isa. 6:3; Hab. 2:14); and the will of God shall be done "*on earth, as it is done in heaven.*"

Daniel's statement, that God's Kingdom will be set up, not after these kingdoms of earth are dissolved, but in their days, while they still exist and have power, and that it is God's Kingdom which shall break in pieces and consume all these kingdoms (Dan. 2:44), is worthy of our special consideration. So it was with each of these beastly governments: it existed before it acquired universal dominion. Babylon existed long before it conquered Jerusalem and

A comparison of early and late editions of Russell's *The Time is at Hand* (those used were dated 1906 and 1920) shows that the attempt to salvage the 1914 failure produced a second failure.

**Figure 8**

1914; and that that date will be the farthest limit of the rule of imperfect men. And be it observed, that if this is shown to be a fact firmly established by the Scriptures, it will prove:—

Firstly, That at that date the Kingdom of God, for which our Lord taught us to pray, saying, "Thy Kingdom come," will have obtained full, universal control, and that it will then be "set up," or firmly established, in the earth

Secondly, It will prove that he whose right it is thus to take the dominion will then be present as earth's new Ruler; and not only so, but it will also prove that he will be present for a considerable period before that date; because the overthrow of these Gentile governments is directly caused by his dashing them to pieces as a potter's vessel (Psa. 2:9; Rev. 2:27), and establishing in their stead his own righteous government.

Thirdly, It will prove that some time before the end of A. D. 1914 the last member of the divinely recognized Church of Christ, the "royal priesthood," "the body of Christ," will be glorified with the Head; because every member is to reign with Christ, being a joint-heir with him of the Kingdom, and it cannot be fully "set up" without every member.

Fourthly, It will prove that from that time forward Jerusalem shall no longer be trodden down of the Gentiles, but shall arise from the dust of divine disfavor, to honor; because the "Times of the Gentiles" will be fulfilled or completed.

Fifthly, It will prove that by that date, or sooner, Israel's blindness will begin to be turned away; because their "blindness in part" was to continue only "until the fulness of the Gentiles be come in" (Rom. 11:25), or, in other words, until the full number from among the Gentiles, who are to be members of the body or bride of Christ, would be fully selected.

Sixthly, It will prove that the great "time of trouble such

1914; and that that date will see the disintegration of the rule of imperfect men. And be it observed, that if this is shown to be a fact firmly established by the Scriptures, it will prove:—

Firstly, That at that date the Kingdom of God, for which our Lord taught us to pray, saying, "Thy Kingdom come," will begin to assume control, and that it will then shortly be "set up," or firmly established, in the earth, on the ruins of present institutions.

Secondly, It will prove that he whose right it is to take the dominion will then be present as earth's new Ruler; and not only so, but it will also prove that he will be present for a considerable period before that date; because the overthrow of these Gentile governments is directly caused by his dashing them to pieces as a potter's vessel (Psa. 2:9; Rev. 2:27), and establishing in their stead his own righteous government.

Thirdly, It will prove that some time before the end of the overthrow the last member of the divinely recognized Church of Christ, the "royal priesthood," "the body of Christ," will be glorified with the Head; because every member is to reign with Christ, being a joint-heir with him of the Kingdom, and it cannot be fully "set up" without every member.

Fourthly, It will prove that from that time forward Jerusalem shall no longer be trodden down of the Gentiles, but shall arise from the dust of divine disfavor, to honor; because the "Times of the Gentiles" will be fulfilled or completed.

Fifthly, It will prove that by that date, or sooner, Israel's blindness will begin to be turned away; because their "blindness in part" was to continue only "until the fulness of the Gentiles be come in" (Rom. 11:25), or, in other words, until the full number from among the Gentiles, who are to be members of the body or bride of Christ, would be fully selected.

Sixthly, It will prove that the great "time of trouble such

A comparison of the early and late editions of Russell's *The Time is at Hand* (those used were dated 1906 and 1920) shows the attempt to salvage the 1914 failure.

**Figure 9**

152          "THE TRUTH SHALL MAKE YOU FREE"

together the three great periods of time from
Adam's creation onward, we get the following
table:

From Adam's creation
to the Flood                 was   1,656 years
From the Flood to the
Abrahamic covenant    was      427 years
From the Abrahamic cove-
nant to end of B.C. 1    was   1,945 years
                                        ─────────
From Adam's creation to
the end of B.C. 1          was   4,028 years

Thereafter the so-called *Anno Domini* or *A.D.*
period began.

From the beginning of A.D. 1, or Year of the
Lord 1, to the beginning of A.D. 1944 is 1,943
full years, which, being added to the above
table, give the time measurement from Adam's
creation to date:

From Adam's creation to
the end of B.C. 1          was  . 4,028 years
From beginning of A.D. 1
to the end of 1943        is    1,943 years
                                        ─────────
From Adam's creation to
the end of 1943 A.D.    is    5,971 years

We are therefore near the end of six thousand years of human history, with conditions
upon us and tremendous events at hand foreshadowed by those of Noah's day.—Luke
17:26-30.

With the publication of *The Truth Shall Make You Free* in 1943, attention was shifted from the 1941 view that the nearness of Armageddon
could be stated in terms of months, to the calculation that 6,000 years
from Adam's creation would be completed in 1972. The publication of
*Life Everlasting—in Freedom of the Sons of God* in 1966, presented a
new calculation that the 6,000 years would run until 1975.

## A SELECTIVE BIBLIOGRAPHY OF MATERIALS
## FOR FURTHER STUDY AND DISTRIBUTION

### Books

Dencher, Ted. *Why I Left Jehovah's Witnesses.* Fort Washington, Pa.: Christian Literature Crusade, 1966.
Presents the writer's testimony and a scriptural refutation of several key Witness doctrines.

Duncan, Homer. *Heart to Heart Talks with Jehovah's Witnesses.* Lubbock, Texas: Missionary Crusader, Inc., 1972.
This work presents "the doctrines of the Jehovah's Witnesses compared with the Holy Scriptures."

Gruss, Edmond C. *Apostles of Denial: An Examination and Exposé of the History, Doctrines and Claims of the Jehovah's Witnesses.* Nutley, N. J.: Presbyterian and Reformed Publishing Co., 1970.
A 324-page book which deals with the Witnesses in a comprehensive way.

————. *The Jehovah's Witnesses and Prophetic Speculation.* Nutley, N. J.: Presbyterian and Reformed Publishing Co., 1972.
Presents an examination and refutation of the Witnesses' position on the second "coming" of Christ in 1914, Armageddon, and the "end of the world."

Hoekema, Anthony A. *The Four Major Cults.* Grand Rapids: Wm. B. Eerdmans Publishing Co., 1963 (pp. 223-371).
A scholarly presentation of the Witnesses' theology and a refutation of their denials on the deity of Christ and eternal punishment. The section on the Jehovah's Witnesses is also published as a separate book titled *Jehovah's Witnesses* (Eerdmans).

Martin, Walter R., and Norman H. Klann. *Jehovah of the Watch Tower*. Sixth Revised edition, 1963; Grand Rapids: Zondervan Publishing House, 1953.

No longer in print but found in many libraries. A totally revised and updated edition written by Dr. Martin was published by Moody Press in 1974. Much of the material in the earlier edition is found in *The Kingdom of the Cults* (Minneapolis, Minn.: Bethany Fellowship, 1965), pp. 34-110.

Schnell, William J. *Thirty Years a Watch Tower Slave*. Grand Rapids: Baker Book House, 1956.

Contains the author's experiences and his interpretation on the inner workings of the Society. Also published in a condensed edition.

Thomas, F. W. *Masters of Deception*. Grand Rapids: Baker Book House, 1970.

Examines and refutes the Witnesses' major doctrinal errors. Contains a helpful Scripture index of references discussed.

Tomsett, Valerie. *Released from the Watchtower*. Fort Washington, Pa.: Christian Literature Crusade, 1971.

An English housewife explains why she is no longer associated with the Witnesses.

Whalen, William J. *Armageddon Around the Corner*. New York: The John Day Company, 1962.

This fairly comprehensive book by a Catholic journalist deals with the history, doctrines, organization, and schisms of the group. He leaves refutation of doctrine to others. Interesting and informative.

## Booklets

Barnett, Maurice. *Jehovah's Witnesses* (Vol. 1). Phoenix, Ariz.: Church of Christ (1606 W. Indian School Road, Phoenix 85015).

Written and published by a Church of Christ pastor. Contains helpful presentations on the history, organization, and doctrines of the Jehovah's Witnesses and a further section on the deity of Christ.

Bruce, F. F., and W. J. Martin. *The Deity of Christ.* Manchester: North of England Evangelical Trust, 1965.

This booklet on the deity of Christ, written by two Bible scholars, is one of the best presentations on the subject. A number of favorite Arian texts are refuted in a note at the rear (pp. 21-24).

Martin, Walter R. *Jehovah's Witnesses.* Minneapolis, Minn.: Bethany Fellowship, 1957.

This booklet contains material from *Jehovah of the Watch Tower.* It is helpful as an orientation on the movement.

Metzger, Bruce M. *The Jehovah's Witnesses and Jesus Christ.* Reprinted in pamphlet form from the April, 1953, issue of *Theology Today.*

Deals with the Witnesses' doctrine of Christ on their own grounds and from their own New World Translation. Available from the Theological Book Agency, Princeton, N. J. 08540.

## Sources of Materials

1. F. W. Thomas, P. O. Box 2784, Vancouver, B. C., Canada.
   Book: *Masters of Deception* (162 pp.)   $2.75 postpaid.
   Tracts: Mr. Thomas publishes a number of tracts exposing the errors of the Witnesses.

2. Homer Duncan, Missionary Crusader, 4606 Avenue H, Lubbock, Texas 79404.
   Book: *Heart to Heart Talks with Jehovah's Witnesses* (156 pp.)   $1.50 postpaid.
   Booklets: Mr. Duncan has written several booklets, and he has published the testimony *From Darkness to Light* by ex-Witness Dennis R. Jackson. It is 20 cents postpaid.

3. Ted Dencher, P. O. Box 199, Sharon, Pa. 16146.
   Book: *Why I Left Jehovah's Witnesses* (224 pp.)   $2.50 postpaid in the United States; $1.75 in Canada.

Booklets: The Rev. Dencher has written several small booklets which are available for 20 and 25 cents postpaid. Quantity prices are given.

LP Records: "Is Jesus Jehovah?"; "I Left Jehovah's Witnesses"; "I Accuse Jehovah's Witnesses"; "The Training Program of the Watchtower Society." Records are $3.00 each postpaid.

4. Religion Analysis Service, 902 Hennepin Avenue, Minneapolis, Minn. 55403.

The RAS publishes a "Catalog of books and tracts exposing cults and unscriptural teachings in the light of God's Word." It is free upon request.

5. Kenneth R. Guindon, Pastoral Care Center, 14800 Sherman Way, Van Nuys, Calif. 91405.

Tapes: "Witnessing to Jehovah's Witnesses" (5 tapes, 1 hour each cassette). Contain Mr. Guindon's testimony, the Witnesses' doctrines and a scriptural refutation, examination and refutation of the New World Translation, and witnessing to Jehovah's Witnesses. $8.75 postpaid.

Tract: "New Birth Brings Freedom" (Former Jehovah's Witness for 16 years tells why he left the movement). $2.50 per 100 for the first 100 (postpaid) and $2.00 for each additional 100.

Other materials are being prepared.

6. Department of Apologetics, Los Angeles Baptist College, Newhall, Calif. 91321.

Books: *Apostles of Denial* (324 pp.) $3.00 postpaid; *The Jehovah's Witnesses and Prophetic Speculation* (127 pp.) $2.00 postpaid.

Booklet: *The Deity of Christ*, by F. F. Bruce and W. J. Martin (24 pp.) 8 for $1.00 postpaid.

Tracts and information sheets: All are 8½x11", printed on both sides. Some are folded to make from 4 to 6 pages. $2.50 per 100 for the first 100 (postpaid) and $2.00 for each additional 100. They may be mixed. "Jehovah's Witnesses—A Survey"; "Why a Witness of Jesus Christ—

168

Not a Jehovah's Witness?"; "Delivered From the Jehovah's Witnesses"; "Dealing with Jehovah's Witnesses" (reprint from *Soul Winner's Digest*); "Is the Watchtower Society God's Channel?"; "The Watchtower Society and Prophetic Speculation."

Special offer of the two books, the one booklet, and one of each of the other materials for $4.50 postpaid. Please indicate this offer when ordering.